ON THEIR SIDE

———

BOB STRACHOTA

On Their
Side

HELPING CHILDREN
TAKE CHARGE OF
THEIR LEARNING

NORTHEAST FOUNDATION FOR CHILDREN

ISBN 0-9618636-3-3
Library of Congress catalog card number 95-71980

Second Printing July 1996

Design by Rebecca S. Neimark, Twenty-Six Letters

Northeast Foundation for Children
71 Montague City Road
Greenfield, MA 01301
1-800-360-6332

FOR ELLEN

The best thing for disturbances of the spirit . . . is to learn.
That is the only thing that never fails. You may grow old and
trembling in your anatomies, you may lie awake at night listening
to the disorder of your veins, you may miss your only love and lose
your moneys to a monster, you may see the world about you
devastated by evil lunatics, or know your honor trampled in the
sewers of baser minds. There is only one thing for it then—to learn.
Learn why the world wags and what wags it.

T. H. WHITE

A question ain't really a question if you know the answer too.

JOHN PRINE

CONTENTS

ACKNOWLEDGEMENTS

———

HOW MANY TEACHERS DOES IT TAKE TO WRITE A BOOK?
Well, I can't imagine what this one would be like if my friends and colleagues hadn't been ready to discuss, encourage, and debate at every step along the way. Like the children I teach, I needed to be both supported and challenged, and I was lucky enough to have people around me who were experts at both.

I am especially grateful to:

Ellen Doris for believing that I could write long before I actually could and for dropping whatever she was doing to puzzle things out with me whenever I said I was stuck.

Mary Beth Forton for setting me straight at the start about the right tone and for being so precise about what she liked and didn't like.

Ruth Charney for championing my efforts and prodding me to do better.

Roxann Kriete for her enthusiasm, insights, and frankness.

Deborah Porter for articulating several years ago two of the guiding ideas in the book—"real questions" and "getting on the child's side."

Nancy Ratner for her patience in helping my ideas grow, her clear perspective, and for helping me to tame the words.

Jane Stephenson for helping me keep my other responsibilities on a leash and for thoughtful and thorough reading.

Patty Lawrence and Sally Kitts for their full and rich commentary on every page.

Joan Strachota for being both clear and blunt.

Sharon Dunn for being supportive throughout the project.

Jim Hauser for believing and reading.

Terry Kayne for tolerating me during the difficulties of the research phase.

Marlynn Clayton for teaching me about being positive and clear and thus helping me move from being a mediocre teacher to a good one.

Mary Ann Minard, Marian Ferguson, Roxanne King, Gean Gow, Linda Hefferman, Marion Da Grossa, Diane Korza,and Julie Sawyer for reading some very raw writing and offering their thoughts.

Chip Wood for believing in the project when it seemed like it was dead in the water.

Jared Hilliker, Alex Mitchel, Joel Strachota, Josh Stuckey, Abby McGuigan, Amber Gurley-Campolo and Carina Koury-Jones whose wonderful drawings bring children to these pages in ways that my words couldn't.

Joel and Gabe for putting up with a father who complained too much when the project refused to wind down.

All of the teachers and parents who have shared their joys and struggles with me over the years.

While writing this book I taught at Greenfield Center School, the laboratory school of Northeast Foundation for Children. NEFC is a private, nonprofit, educational foundation which works to improve the quality of elementary teaching. I am grateful to NEFC for making available the time and resources for me to work on this project.

My biggest debt is to the children that I have taught. In this book I have changed the names and some of the identifying characteristics of the children.

INTRODUCTION

———

A SEVEN-YEAR-OLD ONCE SAID TO ME, "I LIKE THE WAY YOU teach soccer. You're always in the middle, but not in the way." He had captured what I try to do in all my teaching. I want to inspire the children I teach to be passionate about untangling the mysteries of numbers and spiders and history, and also to care deeply about sorting through the problems of how to be fair and kind. I know, however, that the children are the only ones who can create their understanding of how the world works and of how to do the right thing. So while I put myself in the middle of their efforts, I also try not to be in the way. This book is about my attempts to learn to do these two things at the same time.

I have written here about both academic and social learning. I have found that what I figure out about one area often applies to the other as well. For example, when I tried a new way of teaching math, I discovered a whole different way of thinking about how to help children work on solving the problems they have with each other. Vivian Paley (1990) wrote this about the connection between social and academic learning: "Learning to know one another, we develop the logical and emotional precedents required for all other studies" (p. 106). Learning seems to be learning, whether it's about subtraction or dragonflies or kindness or impulse control.

More of the stories in this book deal with social, emotional, and motivational issues than with academic ones. I have weighted things in this direction in order to address the imbalance in our training as teachers, which has always heavily emphasized the academic. I believe that the kind of problem solving which involves children's upsets, joys, compulsions, and furies is as central to their learning as solving the problems of spelling and adding and writing, so I have highlighted that side of the teaching job.

CHAPTER I

How Should

I Teach?

TALES FROM

MUD SEASON

HOW SHOULD I TEACH? UNTIL THE LAST SEVERAL YEARS, the answers that I have come up with most frequently have centered around telling and doing. I have told children what I know or I have told them what they should or shouldn't do. I used these two strategies whether I was teaching multiplication or trying to get a child to do her work or trying to stop her from teasing. Over the past few years I've been experimenting with some different ways to help children learn and grow. Two stories help show where these efforts have led me.

These two stories come from March of a year that I was teaching second graders. I've always thought that it would be nice as a teacher to be able to go straight from February to April. I know that March brings warmth to Washington, D. C. and flowers to Texas, but where I teach in New England, March has no charm. Snow lurks around the parking lot in gritty little clumps and the children and I have been inside for so long that the classroom often starts to seem like a pinball machine. The pent-up energy that comes with this season booby traps far too many of our enterprises. March plays an important part in these two stories.

In our school the children eat lunch in their classrooms. I have a break at this time. One day deep in March, the regular lunch teacher was sick and my second graders had a substitute. After lunch on this day, instead of our usual independent reading, a guest teacher was going to lead the children in a writing exercise.

As I entered the room after my break, the substitute lunch teacher threw up her hands hopelessly, mumbled something I couldn't hear over the noise and left. The reasons for her distress were clear. Jose and Megan were zooming in one direction, Rocky was zipping in another, and there was a group wrestling on the rug where the writing exercise was to take place. Remember that this was March and then add a teacher in a very bad mood. I try to stay positive when I'm teaching, or at least to stay level, but my status as an ordinary human being sometimes weights my mood toward the grumpy end of the scale. This particular week I was feeling a lot of pressure both at work and at home and it made me quite ready to be sour. I was also embarrassed in front of the guest teacher, who was standing off to the side watching my unruly class. As I looked about, my one burning wish was for immediate order. I wondered how I could help the group pull back from chaos.

I rang the bell—my method for getting the whole class's attention. I told them that it was clear to me that they didn't remember how to change from one activity to another, so we would practice it. I had them all return to the places where they had eaten lunch. I asked how they would get to the rug for the writing session and got several appropriate responses. I told them to go ahead and do it. Caitlin bumped Andy on the way to the rug. I rang the bell again. My voice was angry now.

"I know that this isn't the greatest time of the year. I know you're all feeling bouncy. But we have to deal with this problem better. So we are going to practice this again."

I had them return to their lunch places. I asked again how they would get to the rug. They answered. They did it. A very stiff writing session followed. Cleanup at the end of the day was very wired—the pinball effect. I loudly called several misbehaving children to task. I left school that day wondering what had gone wrong.

The younger children in our school have a snack in the morning, but one day in March for some reason it wasn't available. The absence of this nurturing routine ratcheted the March discontent up a notch. I tried quickly to think of a soothing substitute and in desperation I hit on going outside for ten minutes. Of course, right then the playground, which was grass at many times of the year, was made of pure brown goo, so we were forced to a tiny grit and sand-covered corner of the parking lot.

As much as they needed an outlet, I needed a breather, so I wasn't able to summon the energy to organize and run a game. I told them that this corner of the parking lot would be their outside space today and that they could play what they wanted. I turned them loose and hoped for the best.

A half-hearted tag game soon gave way to a far more engaging turf battle. One group seized the high ground, five concrete steps that led into the school. The recently departed two foot snow cover had allowed this group to devise very safe ways to engage in physical struggle during the winter. As I watched now, I could see that they were unaware that the world was no longer cushioned and that physical struggle would very likely lead to blood and tears. Disasters were only barely being avoided.

The need for safety, the need for an outlet, and their love for their game were all at war here. What should I do? I called the group together. I told them that no one had gotten hurt yet, but that there wasn't any snow to protect them and that I'd seen some shoving and that I was worried. I showed them the scars on my left knee from having rounded first base too sharply on the playground when I was in sixth grade. I said that I knew that we needed to be outside and that they seemed to love the game they were playing. I asked if they had any ideas how they could keep playing the game and also keep the blood inside their veins.

They were very ready with opinions.

"The trouble is because the bulldogs are attacking the steps," said Andy.

3

"But that's their job," Caitlin countered. "They sneak up and attack us and we try to keep them out."

"The bull dogs should have their own base," Francisca said.

"Then it would be just like separate houses," James responded. "That's not fun."

Rocky said, "We could walk instead of run."

"That's no fun," Caitlin objected.

Maria said, "How about if when you hold up both hands right in front of someone, they would have to run away?"

"Yeah," said Chuck.

"Good idea," said James.

I said they could call it "electric hands." They squealed their pleasure at this foolish notion. I told them to go try it. Squealing "electric hands," they continued their game—bloodlessly.

THE GOAL—INVENTING UNDERSTANDING

My search for answers to the question of how I should teach revolves around what I think about how people learn. My reactions to these two groups of unruly children show that I can come up with some very different answers on this issue. At the lunch transition I assumed that the children would learn how to solve their problem by being told what to do about it. I assumed that the children playing on the steps would learn if we wondered together about the problem. Eleanor Duckworth (1991) tells a story which sheds light on these two different attitudes.

> My favorite radio show is "A Hitchhiker's Guide to the Galaxy." In one episode, a computer is built expressly for the purpose of answering the question, "What is the meaning of life, the universe, and everything?" When it is ready, they ask it if it can answer the question. It says, yes, it can, but that it will take, as I

recall, seven million years. They say, "Well, OK, go to it." Seven million years later, whoever is around goes to learn the answer. The computer says that it does have the answer, but that it might be a little disappointing. "No, no," they say, "go ahead, what is it?" "Forty-two," the computer says. (P. 7)

To me this story says that unless we go through the complexities of struggle and invention, our knowing is empty. If this is true, then I cannot transfer my knowledge and experience to the children whom I teach. Instead I have to find ways to help children take responsibility for inventing their own understanding of the world and how to live in it. To do this I have to struggle against both my training and my instincts which strongly urge me to be directive: to tell children what I know, to tell them what to do. On the day of the ugly lunch transition, I didn't win that struggle against my directive impulse. When I was faced with widespread unruly behavior, I reverted to management techniques which I had previously found wanting and had been trying to change. I had the children verbalize and practice the "right" behaviors, based on the theory that understanding comes downstream from doing. Over the past few years, I had been re-examining my notions about this way of teaching. I had decided that though children often came to understand through doing, this only happened when the doing was combined with struggle and reflection. I began to see that I had come to rely too exclusively on the doing. So I had started trying, as often as I could, to wonder with children about what to do about a problem, to have them share in the responsibility of creating a solution instead of telling them what to do.

There are still many times when I just tell children what to do. Pace and spirit have a very large effect on learning and I can't always be interrupting our momentum to ponder problems with the children. I also choose to be directive when I judge that it is the best way to get a child to learn or try something difficult or new. In my own learning, I sometimes have to "make" myself do new or hard things. Even when I tell children what to do, however, I want them to reflect and discuss before they begin, and especially afterwards.

The instinct simply to be directive is very strong in me. But when I tell children what to do at the expense of wondering with them, their capacity to assume real responsibility for their actions is diminished. Being directive also obstructs my view of the varied dynamics that are at play in any situation. To put it another way, I have come to believe that leaping into action tends to stop thought for both the teacher and the learner, and without struggle and reflection to back up the doing, the learning becomes hollow.

THE MEANS—WONDERING TOGETHER
AND SHARING RESPONSIBILITY

So my answer to the dilemma of how I should teach has changed. Since we seem to learn largely by constructing our knowledge for ourselves and since this inventing has to involve both doing and reflection, I believe learning must come downstream of a *mix* of doing and wondering; and I've found that it is frequently more effective to start with the reflection and discussion instead of the action.

The way that I handled the chaotic transition from lunch shows what can happen when I choose telling over wondering. When I came into the room, I immediately prescribed action by telling the children to practice moving from one place to another. My action orientation blocked me from seeing that knowing how to move through the room wasn't so much the issue; rather it centered around learning how to wait while carrying the pent-up energy of the cabin fever season.

Rowdy behavior was causing the problems in both the lunch transition and the playground situation, but they ended very differently, because on the playground I had the children share the responsibility for devising the solution instead of creating it for them. In similar situations in the past, I have been much more directive:

• I have given a "time out" to anyone whose play looked too risky.
• I've said, "You are too wild for this to work today. We'd better go in before someone gets hurt."
• I've said, "Your game seems too dangerous to me. I'll help get a game of Circle Name Tag going."
• I've said, "This game looks like fun, but it's sloppy and hard out here. So now we'll have a no touching rule to be sure that no one accidently gets knocked over."
• I've had the children practice moving safely.
• I've gotten mad.

On this particular March morning my experience told me to try a different approach. I was still very directive, but I did not tell the children what to do. I insisted that *they* figure out what to do, that they take responsibility for inventing a solution to the problem. The tool I used to help them was to pose a riddle for us to wonder about together: How could we take into account the need to be outside, their love of their game, and the difficulty of playing it safely in this space? In this wondering they quickly moved from blaming to deliberating about possible solutions. They were inventive and judicious, they fully embraced an ingenious idea, and they proceeded to play with enthusiasm and care.

THE LEVER—ASKING REAL QUESTIONS

The key to helping the children take charge of their learning in this situation was the riddle. Just how central such dilemmas are to learning became clear to me one day when I was visiting a school with my fellow teacher, Deborah Porter, and several other colleagues. The teachers of the school that we were visiting had, over the years, attended several workshops which I had led. They had put into place in their school many of the ideas and techniques which they had learned in these workshops. As my colleagues and I moved from classroom to classroom observing, I found myself becoming puzzled and then upset. Something was wrong here. Though many proven teaching methods were being used, the classrooms, the interactions, and the learning lacked vitality, but I couldn't tell why. Toward the end of the morning I leaned over to Deborah and whispered, "What's wrong here?" Without hesitating, she answered, "No one has asked a real question yet."

This notion of real questions defined wonderfully for me the tool that I had found most useful in helping children learn— whether I was helping them invent ways to add 34 and 79 or create ways to talk in a more friendly way. I've come to define a real question as one which engages the teacher and the learner in exploring the mysteries of the universe, rather than one which engages the learner in exploring the mysteries of what the teacher wants her to say or know or do. If my class is rowdy at a transition, I can ask the children how they should move in the room; or I can explore with them how we could wait peacefully and use energy at the same time. The latter question engages the mind and passion of the class and the teacher. It helps us both to wonder about the space between what we know and what we don't know; it helps the children take charge and invent. Using real questions as the core of my teaching I am continually fascinated by the dilemmas of life and am able to offer them to my students as intriguing and meaty problems.

THE PREREQUISITE—ALLYING WITH THE CHILDREN

The idea of posing a problem instead of a solution seems a simple technical enterprise; but if we look again at the playground situation and the lunch transition, we find that it isn't quite as simple as it seems. In the playground situation I was able to present the children with a real question to chew over because I was first able to ally with them—to understand them and to believe in their goodness. When I saw that their snack was missing I understood that their routine, so soothing to seven-year-olds, had been upset and that they needed a replacement. When I saw them begin to play, I understood that they still had their winter snow-play habits. I believed both that their turf battle game was meaningful and important to them and that they could work out a way to play it safely.

At the lunch transition I had no question for the children to work on because I didn't make the effort to ally with them. Their routines had also been interrupted: they had a different lunch teacher and a change in their after-lunch schedule—all on top of the March heebie-jeebies. I had not believed in them enough to see that there might be a reasonable need behind their behavior and that I might be able to help them find a way to meet that need.

Not only had I ignored what was going on for the children, I had ignored what was going on for me, too. Perhaps if the guest teacher hadn't been there, my system would not have short-circuited and I would have been aware that the whale of my discontent was breaching and so would have been able to do something about it. But the presence of other teachers or visitors calls forth a voice in me that says, "If your class isn't in order, they'll think you're a lousy teacher." In the presence of peers I have to work hard to keep knowing that order is only the necessary substratum for the vitality of thought and interaction that I treasure in a classroom. This day my embarrassment over the chaos tipped the emotional scales and I went blank and could think only of action.

One of the great things about elementary school is that, like baseball, there's always another game the next day. So that evening after I had worked to see the situation from their perspective and had understood why I had acted the way I did, I could understand that the problem had more to do with waiting than moving.

Having gotten to this better point, I still woke up early the next morning feeling more exhaustion, pressure, and irritation than clarity. I had an early morning meeting and when I came into the classroom in mid-morning it looked very similar to the scene from the day before when I had come in after lunch. The children had just finished a science lesson that had clearly not gone smoothly. Nick, a particularly live wire, had been banished from the room and other children were bopping and jiving in many directions. I rang the bell and told them that we would have a meeting before we started math.

I started the meeting by talking about my irritability. Had they noticed? Of course, they had. "Some examples, please." Lots of examples. "Have you ever had other irritable teachers?" Lots of examples. Just as in the "electric hands" situation, when I had put my worry and knee scars on the table, I was now making my bad mood a conscious part of what was happening in our classroom. I told them that I didn't like it when I taught while feeling grouchy, that I'd try to be more cheerful, and that they might be able to help in some way.

I asked if they had noticed anything besides my grouchiness that was different about my teaching yesterday afternoon.

"You were telling us what to do more," Kate said.

"How was that different from what I usually do?" I asked.

Sarah said, "Usually you make us figure out what to do about a problem."

I said that I thought that a lot of the problem yesterday had to do with March energy and having to wait between activities. I pointed out that the main place that they had to wait was on the rug and I asked if they had any ideas how they could use energy in inside ways and wait at the same time. I asked that they try to think of things that would be fun, because it helped me be more cheerful when I saw kids having fun. The suggestions flowed: dancing to taped music, gentle head butting, arm wrestling, and so on. They voted for arm wrestling. We set up protocols. We went on to a productive math session. Transitions went smoothly for the rest of the grim mud season. Once I had been able to get on the children's side, I was able to present the situation as a challenging dilemma and they were able to devise a clever solution.

TEACHING CHILDREN TO TAKE RESPONSIBILITY

In considering the problem of how I should teach, I first had to become clear about my goal. My goal is to help children take responsibility for inventing their own understanding of how the world works and of how to live ethically. To achieve my goal I center my teaching around three practices:

I ally with the children

I have to get on the children's side. To accomplish this I have to 1) *believe* that children are good and hunt out and appreciate that goodness, even when it seems resolutely hidden away; 2) *understand* what is going on for *them*; and 3) *understand* what is going on for *myself*.

I ask real questions

The empathy and understanding I gain from allying help me to understand the dilemma of the situation so that I can formulate and pose real questions.

I share responsibility

The real questions stimulate my students and me to wonder together about the world and its problems. In these discussions I set high expectations about the children inventing their own understanding and making responsible choices about what to do.

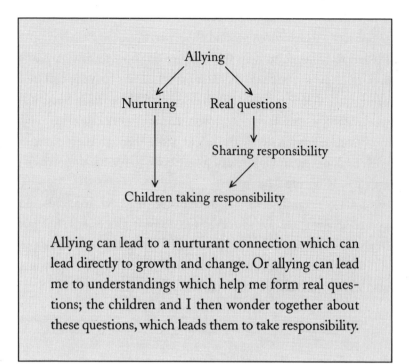

Allying

Nurturing   Real questions

Sharing responsibility

Children taking responsibility

Allying can lead to a nurturant connection which can lead directly to growth and change. Or allying can lead me to understandings which help me form real questions; the children and I then wonder together about these questions, which leads them to take responsibility.

I feel that it is necessary to say one more thing before going on. Believing in the goodness of children, allying with them, listening carefully to them, and wondering with them could lead to a permissiveness that would corrode true learning and growth if I did not employ my authority to be sure that these tools are used in the service of my ultimate goal: that the children take respon- sibility for their learning and behavior. I can only wonder with children and learn from them if I am first fully in charge of my classroom. I do this by making sure that my expectations are high and clear. The children know that I will listen to their needs, but they also know that I will be demanding of them. Maintaining high standards around the central goal of children taking responsibility ensures that my classroom will be the opposite of permissive. I ally with children around their needs, not just their wants. I listen to children to help them figure out how to solve a problem, not how to evade the hardest part. I expect that the children in my care will think through hard equations, turn in beautiful work, learn to stop themselves from hitting, work quietly while I am having a conference with a child, work through their quarrels with each other, and figure out a way both to wait and to use energy inside during March.

I am constantly trying both to expect the best from children and to accept them for who they are, to be in the middle but not in the way. I believe that in the stories throughout this book you will see the kind of authority that is necessary for this stretching and allying to work hand in hand.

CHAPTER 2

From Outlaws

To Leaders

A RIDDLE

AT A STAFF MEETING IN EARLY SEPTEMBER ONE YEAR, A fifth/sixth grade teacher said, "There's too much testosterone at work during soccer. My sixth grade boys are just too unruly and we've got to find some way to knock it out of them."

We fifth/sixth grade teachers had decided to run the soccer program ourselves that year and frustration was mounting on all sides. In the past we had hired real coaches, but that had never worked very well. After many years we realized that we were asking these coaches to do something that they weren't trained to do. Their experience and skills were geared to teaching soccer to voluntary players. Our program was not voluntary: *all* of our fifth and sixth graders play because we believe that there is a tremendous amount to be learned from working together on this complex sport. Each year there are children who have never played before, some who have played a little and don't like the sport all that much, and some who are "gung ho". We had been asking these coaches to teach to all these levels, and, of course, to make it be fun as well. After several unsuccessful years we thought that maybe it would work better if we tried to do it ourselves. So what if we didn't know that much about soccer? We knew the individual children and we knew how to teach. We'd fake the rest.

I volunteered to organize the program. My knowledge of soccer is very rudimentary, but when I taught second grade I had figured out a way of organizing the game that had always kindled great enthusiasm in the seven-year-olds. I imagine that quite a few readers of this book have minimal interest in soccer, some perhaps even viewing it as just a bunch of kids running around. But I ask those readers to suspend these notions for a bit. Over my years of teaching soccer to second graders, I have come to see the sport as an incredibly rich learning situation. I have seen timid children find their fierce side and egocentric children see the benefit of contributing to the group. Children have learned how to keep competitiveness from dominating and how to get over their fear of competing. They have learned how to communicate about things they don't like, how to appreciate each other's efforts, and how to be good winners and losers. Children have tried something completely new and found out that they loved it. I have seen children become physically stronger, deal with pain and frustration, take pride in their improvement and in their team. In soccer, children have fulfilled the main goals that I have for them: they have learned to work hard, feel good about themselves, and treat each other well. And they have had fun to boot.

When I took on the fifth/sixth grade soccer program, I had in my head that rich picture of the learning that the sport had prompted in my second graders. I set out to see how to make the same things happen with the older children. I sought counsel with a teacher who ran a highly successful and very egalitarian junior high school soccer program. I worked at adapting her ideas to our younger children. I learned drills. I got help in running a workshop for the fifth and sixth grade teachers who would be doing the coaching. On the third day of school we were ready to roll.

The first drill that I ran was much too complex and failed miserably. It was downhill from there. After a week, a mutiny was afoot amongst the older boys. They had gone to soccer camps for years. They knew the game well and loved it; they felt that we teachers didn't know what we were doing. They particularly chafed at the drills designed to teach them to hold position laterally on the field. Though this is in fact a necessary soccer skill, it was new to them. They were especially motivated in regard to scoring, of course, and they found it very confining to have to follow a strategy that limited them to playing on only a third of the field. We were emphasizing this skill early on so that the less skilled players would have more of a chance to get the ball. But, though those less experienced players were getting the ball a good deal of the time, any possibility that they would develop some enthusiasm for the game was being undermined by the surliness and aggression of these more skilled boys. These boys had become the rotten apples that were spoiling the bushel. Whenever there was an opportunity to score, they left their zone and overran the weaker players. When spoken to or disciplined for this, they kicked the ground, grumbled oaths, and talked back. They carried on loudly before, during and after practices about not being allowed to play the "right" way. My visions of joyful growth through sport had been replaced by an ugly contest over rules and rights.

I knew that things would only get worse when I announced the method that I had devised to make certain that everyone would have a chance to play their best at their own level. The structure that I had come up with was that the stronger players would be restricted not only to a third of the field laterally, but also to half of the field lengthwise. I knew that the strong players would completely rebel against this idea because, first of all, this *truly* is not the way soccer is officially played and, secondly, it was a modification of the three section system that I had used with my second graders and so it would be seen as infantile. I also knew that even third grade teachers had had no luck in trying to implement my notion of dividing the playing field so that children would play only against those of similar strength and skill levels. My huge list of goals for this enterprise now seemed hopelessly idealistic.

We teacher/coaches met. There were lots of suggestions about what to do: make it a penalty for a player to leave her zone; appeal to the sixth grade boys to play less ferociously; read those boys the riot act; develop a reward system for generously muted play; ask those boys to "adopt" a few players from their team and teach them something that the boys could do particularly well. I said that I would think these suggestions over and meet with the boys the next day.

That night I thought about all the things that I had seen soccer do for children. None of them were happening with these fifth and sixth graders. Even the most basic thing was missing: I had wanted everybody to be able to feel good about themselves but no one did. And no one was having fun. I thought about the sour boys. They loved soccer tremendously but they were miserable. That seemed very wrong. It didn't help that it was the start of the year and so they were still very much in the stage of jostling for position with each other, trying to prove themselves and get clear about the pecking order. They were also experimenting with the sarcastic attitude of the budding adolescent. Several were extremely competitive as well. All of this meant that they especially needed to be able to shine at this thing in which they were so invested. I thought about my own love of playing hard at sports. I didn't want these boys to play any less fiercely; in fact, I wanted the other children to become as passionate as they were. From these reflections about the children's needs, I formed a notion of the kind of conversation that I wanted to try with the boys.

The next day, I invited them to have lunch with me. The fact that none of them happened to be in my class gave this invitation very much of a summoned-before-the-principal feeling. They sat down, eyeing each other knowingly.

"Do you have any idea why I wanted to meet with you?" I began.

Dylan responded immediately. "Luke, Sal, Mack, Dylan, and Miguel all together. That seems like trouble to me." He grinned a self-satisfied grin at his buddies.

"Yeah, we spell trouble," echoed Luke happily.

"Do you guys get in trouble in your classroom?" I asked.

"Oh, yeah," they chorused, snickering.

"Well, it's not trouble this time," I said. The smiles slowly dropped off their faces as they eyed me, trying to puzzle out what else it could be. "I've got a problem that I can't figure out," I continued, "and I'd like your help."

"Oh, I get it," Dylan said. "We're your problem—in soccer." His eyes were twinkling again. He'd been right after all.

"You're right that there's a problem in soccer," I said, "but you're not it." I paused. "Do you agree that there's a problem in soccer?"

"Yeah," Sal said uncertainly.

"I don't see anyone having much fun," I said. "I'm trying to figure out why that is. Do you have any ideas?"

They were very tentative. I encouraged them to tell me what they really thought so that maybe we could figure out a solution. They hedged a bit more. Then Miguel said, "It just doesn't make sense that we shouldn't go in and try to score when we get the ball."

"So you'd like more chances to score," I said.

"Yeah," Sal said. "But if I'm playing wing, Mrs. Williams says I have to stay on the side and not funnel toward the goal. That's what she calls it when I try to score. She says I'm funnelling toward the goal." His words were soaked in scorn.

"The point of the game is to score goals," Dylan said.

"You guys are really good at soccer," I said. "Mack, remember when Rumeal came at you and you stood right in front of him and you both fell over and you came up with the ball?" Mack nodded. "Luke, you have that move when you're dribbling and you crick your foot around the ball so it looks like you're going to go to the right but then you go left. You guys aren't getting to do that kind of stuff enough. Which one of you do you think is the fastest?"

They proceeded with a nice analysis of who was fast, who was good at faking, who was good at defense, and who had a strong kick. It ended up with Mack saying, "See the thing is, we're the most offensive players."

"In the good sense," I said. "I play tennis and I love to play offensively. I try to hit hard and hit to the corners and rush the net. We've got to figure out some way for you to be able to use more of your offensive skills."

"Just let us go anywhere on the field," Sal said.

I felt that the boys knew I understood them now and that they were ready to look at the situation in greater complexity. I said, "I want you guys to be able to do your best stuff out there. I like to watch good players and I like to coach good players. But the problem is that the soccer we do here at school isn't like the leagues or the camps that you play in. The kids there have all played a lot of soccer. A lot of the kids here at school don't play that much. You guys are strong and fast and experienced. If you can go anywhere on the field, you'll just run over a lot of these kids. And that wouldn't be much of a soccer game. But if the other kids had the chance, they might get better. You know soccer better than I do. Maybe you can figure out a way that you can play the way you want to and that will let the others learn to play fiercely, too. I'll just listen for a while while you try to figure something out."

Rarely in such discussions do I put myself as much on the sidelines as I did here, but I felt that the extra autonomy would spur the boys' thinking. They started out trying to segregate teams by skill level, but soon found that there weren't enough strong players for a real game. So they devised and debated and revised several elaborate schemes. Though I did not involve myself at this point in the specifics of what the games would look like, I asked several times whether the strong, the medium, and the weak players would all like the latest plan that they had devised. I tried to keep the boys focused on the fact that this was a right versus right situation. I kept before them the challenge of figuring out a way that everyone could get their apparently contradictory rights met. Once when they were ready to give up, I told them that I couldn't justify taking an hour out of the school day for soccer for the next five weeks unless we could devise something that would work for everyone. In the end they came up with a plan very similar to the one that I had invented but had never discussed with them. We talked about some weaknesses that I saw with their plan and we both compromised.

The next day Dylan and Mack came and asked if they could run a goalie clinic for the teams. I asked them to write a proposal that would describe the drills that they would use, how long each drill would take, how they would choose the participants, and how they would maintain order. I then had the idea that during this clinic—if it actually came about—the other three boys could tutor an individual or two from their team. When I mentioned this to them, they were only lukewarm about the idea. Then I suddenly realized that they could also offer clinics. This idea excited them.

Over the next few days, the five boys used every chance they could to plan their practice. They even convinced their teacher that they should be able to work together on the project during their silent study periods. After a week they submitted detailed drawings and time tables of how the practice would be organized. They envisioned several follow-up clinics.

Their practice came off very well, though hardly flawlessly. The follow-up clinics were never mentioned again, though; the boys apparently decided that the struggles and effort involved in organizing drills was better left to the teachers. The structure which they had invented for the games worked wonderfully and the season was marked by enormous growth in individual and team skills, great pride in these accomplishments, and a spirited camaraderie amongst all the players.

Rarely in my teaching does a situation move as speedily and effectively from problem to resolution as it did in this case. I think that the main reasons for this success were that I got on the boys' side, posed them a challenging riddle, and shared power so that they would really take charge.

SEARCHING FOR THE REAL QUESTION

At the start of this story, the boys' rude and egocentric behavior was thwarting my lovely plan for everyone to enjoy and grow from playing soccer. This behavior was irritating and frustrating, but in this situation I didn't have to think for too long to come up with a pretty good idea of what might be going on. I have taught many boys who, when struggling to succeed academically or trying to fit in socially, have used their physical prowess to feel good about themselves. So I reasoned that these boys needed a place to be able to use their particular kind of strength. Also, I love to play hard and to compete myself, so I understand the power that doing these things can give people. Often my hardest work when I'm trying to understand difficult behaviors is to become clear about the main issue. But here, once I had thought a bit about these boys and in what ways their tendencies resembled my own, the issue came into focus quite readily. The reason that we were playing soccer in the first place was to give all the children the chance to feel in themselves the kind of strength that these boys had. Somehow there had to be a way for the boys to be able to use their strength while the other children found their own.

GETTING ON THEIR SIDE

When the boys entered our meeting reveling in a different kind of strength—their outlaw status—I decided not to mention their obnoxious behavior of the previous week. In my experience, both as a teacher and also in my other relationships, I find that nothing freezes the ability to work productively on a problem like judgment. When I am attacked, my instinctive response is to defend myself. Though there are those who see uses for guilt, I have mostly seen it get in the way. I rarely see reflection or problem solving as the response when someone is blamed. These boys dropped their bravado and became intently serious as soon as it became clear that the blame that they were expecting wasn't going to be there.

Their interest in working on the problem was then heightened by two things. First, they saw that I admired the way they played the game. Because I saw these boys only at soccer time, we hadn't had an opportunity to build a positive relationship and they had little reason to trust me, so it was especially important for me to let them know that they were appreciated. To help with this I made sure that they got the opportunity to carry on a bit about their skills.

Second, they found out that I liked to play their way myself. I have found that nothing galvanizes children's attention more in a conversation than my admission that I have the same propensities, flaws, desires, or impulses as they do. Of course, this admission has to be true, not just some sort of empathic trick. The children will see right through any manipulation. But if I hunt a little,

I can always find some way that I demonstrate the same wayward tendencies that they do. Empathizing in this way is so often what changes my reaction to children from irritation to connection. When I'm frustrated with a disorganized child, I remind myself about the times that I can't find my car keys. When I feel myself becoming angry at a bossy child, I try to remember the times when I've just had to have my own way. Finding similarities to the children does not make me excuse their behavior; rather, it helps both me and them be truly curious about the predicament. In this case it didn't take much hunting to find the common ground. So by this point in the conversation, the boys were feeling that their desires were entirely human. The focus had been on the desires, not on how those wishes had been expressed.

POSING THE QUESTION

Once I saw that the boys knew that I understood their perspective and that I was on their side, I decided that they were ready to consider the problem in its greater complexity. The stage had been set for me to say that I thought that the problem wasn't simply that they were unhappy, because if they got to be happy by having the run of the field, everyone else would be unhappy; and if that were the case, what kind of games could there be? The question was both ethical and practical. How could both kinds of players get what they needed and how could both kinds of players get to play fierce soccer?

Here were riddles to test the minds of these experienced young soccer players. I am always looking for this nasty nub of the matter to challenge our thinking—both mine and the children's. I can best help children take responsibility for their thinking and actions by helping them feel fascinated by life's dilemmas and then helping them feel that they have the power to go to work on these predicaments. (This way of articulating these goals is extrapolated from Ellen Doris's (1991) goals for working with children in science. She writes that her approach is designed to ". . . help children feel interested in the world around them and [be] able to find out about that world" [p. 5].) I have found that if the questions I proffer are real ones, not leading ones, the children develop the desire and the capacity to untangle these intriguing webs. Making the formation of these real questions such a central part of my job helps me resolve the problem of how I should teach. Since I believe that I cannot pass on the part of the truth that I know simply by telling it to a child, I must set up situations which allow her and me to explore together so that she can invent her own understanding. Therefore my job becomes one of looking for the right questions rather than the right answers. (A further advantage of this way of working is that the partial answers which I have developed myself get expanded.)

SHARING POWER

Of course, my job is not finished once I have been able to frame the situation as a provocative riddle. I have said that children will invariably go to work on a juicy problem, but this is true only if I really believe that they can and should be full partners in mulling over and devising a solution to the quandary. For this "real question method" to work, I must be sincere when I enjoin those who have the problem to ponder it and devise its solution. Just as the questions with which I frame the dilemmas must be real, my willingness to share power in the search for answers must also be real. If I have an outcome that I am set on—a hidden agenda—the children will always sniff it out and the search will be dead in the water.

I believe that children who learn in a situation where power is truly shared learn to take charge of their lives. Several years ago a second grader named Sarah spoke eloquently about what this sense of power meant to her. Her comments came up at a Valentine's party. We were trying to improve a little on the *Be Mine* level of friendship on the heart candies by gathering to talk about what we liked about each other. Eventually some of the children got around to saying what they liked about me. Sarah said, "I like how you leave a lot of things up to us." I asked what she meant by that. She gave several examples, ending up with, "We got to figure out how we could have this party so that we would like it and you would like it." Power sharing was very real and important to Sarah and she talked about it in a lovely way—I "left a lot up to them."

In the soccer situation I "left it up to them" more radically than I usually do. I did this because I thought that if I were involved very much in the details of the problem there was a good chance that these boys would wind up wrestling with me rather than with the problem. I still had lots to do though, especially in keeping the boys focused on the heart of the problem that they were trying to solve: how everyone could feel good about playing soccer and get better at it. Things worked out unusually well. It was remarkable to me that the plan the boys came up with was so like my own. The only major difference was that they wanted to be able occasionally to play a position which would have the run of the entire field. My compromising on this seemed a small price for the investment which they now brought to this enterprise. They were pleased to have figured out a way that the games could work and they were thrilled with their idea of the clinics.

TEACHING RESPONSIBILITY—"ETHICAL FITNESS"

My goal with these boys was to help them take responsibility for their behavior and for the problem we all had. One important part of getting there was helping them keep trying when they wanted to quit. Ethical dilemmas like the one confronting these boys require very hard work and we can all benefit from encouragement to stay the course in such situations. Helping children see the rewards that are possible from persevering with such difficult decision-making is part of helping them develop what Rushworth Kidder (1995) calls "ethical fitness" (pp. 57–75). The consequences are serious if we shrink from helping children develop the capacity to tackle the legions of ambiguous situations where our rights are obstructed by and linked to the rights of others. These sixth grade boys knew that the consequence of their not being able to design a fair way to play soccer games would be that those games wouldn't happen. They came to see that their welfare and that of others were inextricably intertwined. I believe that many of the skills that are necessary for solving knotty ethical quandaries are the same as those that are needed for solving the mysteries of math, reading, science. When I put real questions at the center of my curriculum, my students learn to pursue the mysteries of equations, literature, and electricity and also learn to become empathic, to make fair decisions, and to share power—even when the only authority present is our common humanity. The need for these ethical skills in our society is enormous. John Nicholls (1993) writes that, "The stomach for participation in intellectual and ethical controversy is the basis of cultural literacy in an adventurous, democratic society" (p. 180). Those sixth grade boys persevered and thought through a nasty ethical predicament. One of my main tasks in helping children take responsibility is to provide productive opportunities for grappling with such controversy and to help them prize the rewards of seeing such deliberations through.

In the first chapter I listed the practices which underlie my teaching. Here is how the various elements of those practices were at work in this situation:

ALLYING WITH CHILDREN

Believing in children

I believed that the boys' desire to use their power and skill by playing fiercely was worthwhile. I also believed that they could take others' needs into account and change their behavior.

Understanding children

My reflections about the boys led me to think that their low self-esteem combined with their competitiveness, their anti-authority attitudes, and their struggles for dominance were driving them to try to gain attention through resistance to, rather than participation in, their community.

Knowing my similarities

I admire passionate effort and I knew that playing hard gave me great satisfaction and a feeling of my power.

POSING REAL QUESTIONS

I first posed the problem of why no one was having fun at soccer. Later I moved to the question of how both the weak and the strong players could enjoy soccer and play to their full ability.

SHARING RESPONSIBILITY

Wondering together

They debated, devised, and revised; we compromised.

Setting high expectations

I set and continually reinforced the bottom line that any plan had to satisfy the needs of the whole group. I had them stick with their effort when they wanted to give up. I insisted that they thoroughly plan their instructional clinic.

Helping children make responsible choices

I kept the competing needs before the boys and they decided on a very democratic scheme and also volunteered to teach soccer skills to their classmates.

CHAPTER 3

Academics

EXPLORING

THE MYSTERIES

OF NUMBERS,

FROGS, AND

GOVERNMENT

ALTHOUGH I BELIEVE THAT THE SOCIAL SIDE OF LEARNING is as important as the academic, I spend the majority of my time teaching language arts, math, social studies, and science. While I build in opportunities to discuss social issues on a regular basis and make sure that transitions are long enough for me to have conversations with children and alter the schedule when I judge that it's important to deal with a social issue, the bulk of my energy still goes toward academics. Allying, asking real questions, and wondering together guide me in this area of my teaching as much as they do in social matters.

THE MYSTERIES OF NUMBERS

It is math time in my second grade classroom. As I erase the children's various thoughts about 60 plus 60 from the chalk board, twenty-three children wait eagerly to see what will be next. Well, maybe Charlie is playing with his sneakers and Melissa is looking out of the window, but mostly the children are not only attentive at these daily math sessions but are also very enthusiastic. The feeling in the group during these whole class math meetings is similar to what happens when I read them a good mystery— there is the same combination of tension and excitement.

The mystery on this particular day is taking place in a new land: we are beginning to add numbers whose sum will take us into the hundreds. I replace 60 + 60 with 80 + 70 and watch while the children grapple with the issue, relying only on their own thinking—no pencils or paper, no manipulatives. It's a lovely sight, twenty-three children thinking hard. After a bit some hands start to go up. I wait a little while longer and then say to Beth, "Tell us how you are thinking about it."

"I take 30 from the 80 and put it with the 70 to make 100. Then I put the 50 that was left over from the 80 with the 100 and get 150."

While Beth is talking, I translate her ideas onto the chalkboard so that the children can see them as well as hear them:

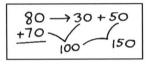

When she has finished, I say, "You always like to look for ways to make 10. Now you're looking for a way to make 100. Did anyone do it a different way?"

Lisa says, "I know that 8 and 7 are 15; but this is 80 and 70 so the 5 of the 15 would have to be 50 and the 10 of the 15 would be 100 so that's 150."

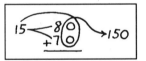

"Nice," I say. "You add the 8 and the 7 and then change them to 80 and 70. Other ways?"

Dan says, "I remembered from the last problem that 60 and 60 are 120; and 70 is 10 more than 60, and 80 is 20 more than 60; so that's 30 more than 120, and that's 150."

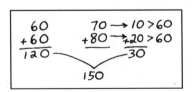

"So your memory helped you get started," I say. "Great job. More?" Many hands go up. "All of you have different ways?" They nod. I call on Jackie.

"Well, I remembered about the 60 and 60 being 120 like Dan did. And since in that one 6 and 6 are 12 and the 2 is a 20, then in this one 8 and 7 are 15 so the 5 will be 50, so it's 150."

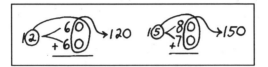

Jesse has a question. "But when the 5 becomes a 50, why isn't the 10 still a 10?"

"Great question," I say. "Anyone like to say what they think?" Several hands go up. "Jesse, pick someone to explain their idea to you." She chooses Emma but Emma gets confused in the middle of her explanation. "This is very hard," I say. "Anyone else like to try?" Jesse chooses Lakeisha.

"The 5 is 5 tens, so that's 50; and the 10 is 10 tens so that's 100; so together they're 150."

"Does that make sense?" I ask Jesse.

"Not really."

"Well, we'll be doing a lot more of these. You keep thinking and listening and I bet it'll get clearer." Then I say to the group, "Let's do a different problem." There is much complaining about this idea. "You mean you want to do this one *more* ways?"

"Yes, yes," they exclaim.

"OK." I call on Chris.

"Well, 50 and 50 are 100. And 80 is 30 more than 50 and 70 is 20 more, so together that's 50 more. You put that 50 on the 100 and you have 150."

More hands go up. "You mean you have *more* ways?!"

"Yes, yes," they exclaim.

"Good," I say. "You can use them on the next problem." There is much groaning. They are just dying to tell all their good ideas.

To my way of thinking, this discussion has the same virtues that the soccer conversation had. The children are intensely curious about what 70 plus 80 could mean; their thinking about solutions is extremely inventive and diverse; they are eager to talk about their ideas and to listen to each other; they are willing to struggle with things they don't understand; and they are very invested—so much so that it is hard to limit their ideas when it is time to move on.

I would be very happy if this eager and resourceful spirit happened in my classroom all day long. The math meetings are one of the places where I can most consistently help children work this way. It has not always been the case that I have been able to foster this level of involvement and creativity in math work. I floundered for years, trying this system and that one, using manipulatives, drills, algorithms, and games. Then I saw Constance Kamii's videotape (1989) about place value and read her book (1989) about second grade mathematics and my skills as a teacher made a quantum leap. Not only my skills at teaching math, but all of my teaching skills. Her *constructivist* thinking about math gave substance to principles that had been rumbling around in me for years, unable to find a way to be articulated or tried. When I began doing math this way I got a crash course in how to become intrigued by children's thinking and how to follow that thinking. I learned how to pose questions and provide situations that would allow children to understand through discussing, thinking, making mistakes, and debating. Soon I was trying to use these techniques everywhere in my teaching, applying the same set of principles to help someone learn about writing or history or how to be friendly and fair that I was using to help them learn to add. It's no wonder that the math meeting about 70 + 80 resembles the soccer discussion.

The heart of constructivist thinking is captured by the title of Piaget's (1973) book, *To Understand Is To Invent*. There is much writing that clearly and thoroughly describes constructivist theory or practice (Fosnot, 1989; Duckworth, 1987, 1991; Kamii, 1985, 1989; Inhelder, Sinclair, Bovet, 1974). My purpose here is to show what this approach has brought to my teaching and how it has affected my belief that real questions are at the center of good teaching and learning.

Let's go back to the discussion of 70 plus 80 and see what made the children so curious, motivated, creative, communicative, and willing to struggle. My role was both very simple and at the same time quite radical.

1) I presented a real problem.
2) I believed that the children would, over time, be able to devise ways to figure out the problem by talking about their thinking with each other.
3) I was fascinated by and enthusiastic about their efforts and wondered along with them.

Asking real questions

Just what was the "real problem" here and why did it hold such power? What I was asking the children to think about was what

37

they knew about the numbers and from that to puzzle out a solution. The "real question" here was, *What do these numbers mean?* In much math instruction the question that the learner is faced with is, *Can you remember the method for solving this problem?* Asking the children to devise their own understanding about what the numbers mean instead of asking them to remember a technique for dealing with the numbers is far more likely to stimulate involvement and thinking. As in the soccer situation, I gave these children a riddle worthy of their full attention. Their task was to duel with reality itself—in this case a number relationship—rather than with someone else's formula for dealing with reality. They were being asked to figure out what they thought, rather than to remember a system.

One reason that this approach to solving math problems captivates children is because it assumes that there are many ways of making sense of these numbers. The fear of being judged for doing things the wrong way doesn't get in the way of the mind's passion to unravel. In the soccer discussion, the boys became willing to get to work on the problem once they understood that they were not being judged and that their view was one of several right ways of looking at the situation. I believe that the same dynamic was at work in this math discussion. These second graders were eager and thoughtful because there wasn't a right way against which their thinking would be measured. They knew that they would be right when they could make sense of the problem.

Believing that children will create solutions

In math, I never ask the children for the answer; instead I ask them to tell how they are thinking about the problem. In doing this I am saying that their thinking is the important thing and that there is ground to be gained from articulating what they are thinking. I am saying, "I believe that you can figure this out. And when it's hard, I believe you'll get clearer as you talk and listen to others' thoughts." The children soon come to believe in their own thinking, especially as they discover how well it can serve them. They even become willing to use it in uncharted waters. The children in this situation had never seen a problem like 80 + 70 before, but they believed that they could make sense out of it and they did. My belief in people's ability to solve problems by talking about them has been greatly increased by this math work. Each year the students in my classes have become proficient mathematicians using this approach.

Being curious about children's thinking

When I pose a real problem and the children go to work on it, my job isn't over once I have let them know that I believe they can figure it out. I can best define what else I must do with two stories.

One day I watched a first grade teacher pose a wonderful math problem and have it go nowhere. She was asking the children for equations which would add up to the day's date. I had seen this question excite children for years because of its challenging and open-ended nature. But this time the reaction was very flat. At first I thought, *This is an extremely even and calm teacher; perhaps she could work on making some of her teaching more dramatic.* Then I realized that for any curriculum to work, the teacher must be fascinated by the intersection made by the content and the learner. Perhaps that first grade teacher was doing the equation work because she had heard that it was a good idea. She did not seem intrigued by what the numbers could do nor did she seem curious about how the children might think about what the numbers could do.

The other story about the importance of teacher curiosity has to do with show and tell, now renamed "sharing." I've included sharing in my morning meetings for a long time because I know that it provides an important bridge to the child's world. I was often bored, however, with the daily recitation about dead guinea pigs and visits to grandmothers, the sharing of action figures and dolls. But my attitude has changed. Now I am always on the hunt for the real question behind even the simplest sharing and I have learned to be truly intrigued by the children's perceptions. Sharing now seems to me to be a very potent intersection between content and learner. Action figures launch discussions about how people use their power, dead guinea pigs lead to discussion about loss.

Doing constructivist math has tuned me in to the pleasures to be found in following a child's thinking and made me very enthusiastic about what happens when a child's mind meets a juicy question. Both the children and I gain enormously from this. I cannot overemphasize the excitement that has been added to teaching for me since I have developed the habit of following children's thinking and figuring out how I can best help as they think. This attitude fills my work with intrigue, challenge, and discovery. I know that $6 + 8 = 14$, but I have no idea how they will come to know this or how I will help them until I ask them what they are thinking and we start talking about it. Teaching has become as thrilling as a good mystery for me.

The children in the discussion about 70 plus 80 were thoughtful and enthusiastic partly because they found it tremendously stimulating and empowering to solve real problems through their own devices and partly because I was intrigued about both the problem and their thinking so I was wondering along with them.

Let's examine what Jesse and some others made of the next problem in math that day. I erased the last idea about 70 plus 80 and said, "I'd like a noun, please."

Kate volunteered, "Witch."

I told a story. "A Bouly-Swag was demolishing the country-side. A witch decided to make a soup to poison it. She put in 6 gallons of swamp water, 34 poison ivy leaves, and 97 frogs. She dipped her finger in and tasted it. 'Aagggh!' she exclaimed. 'Too bitter. He'll never drink this. It needs some toads.' She put in 67 toads. Now it tasted great. How many amphibians does it take to make a tasty Bouly-Swag poison?" While I was telling the story, I wrote on the board:

> 6 gallons swamp water
> 34 poison ivy leaves
> 97 frogs
> 67 toads

The children thought for a while and then I called on Clifford. "I will add the 67 toads to the 97 frogs, because they are the amphibians. I take the 10 from the 60 and put it on the 90 for 100. Then I put the 50 that was left over from the 60 with the 100, and that's 150. Then I put one 7 on for 157. Now I don't know what to do next."

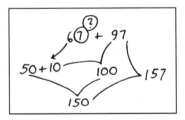

I asked the group, "Any suggestions for Clifford?"

"Wait," Clifford said. "I'll add the two 7s together. That's 14. I'll put it on the 150, and that's 164."

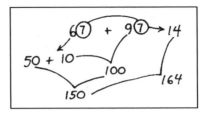

"You figured it out by talking about it," I said to Clifford. "Did any one do it another way?"

Marietta said, "7 and 7 are 14. I do the nines trick with the 9 and the 6, so that's 15. But they're 90 and 60 not 9 and 6 so that would be. . . . That's where I get stuck."

$$15 < \frac{97}{+67} > 14$$

I asked Jesse, "Do you want to try to help out?"

"OK, I'll try. The 5 of the 15 will be 50 so the 15 will be 150. But I don't know what to do with the 7s."

"Do you understand what Jesse did with the 15?" I asked Marietta.

"Not really."

"Why is this 15 really 150?" I asked. "Who will say what they think?"

TJ volunteered. "The 15 came from the 6 and the 9 which are really 60 and 90."

"Does that make sense to you?" I asked Marietta.

"No."

Gwen said, "The 1 is 100 because the 90 is very high so with 60 more it would have to be over 100."

"I still don't get it," Marietta said.

TJ followed up on Gwen's idea. "Six and 9 are 15 but it has to be higher than 15 because the numbers are higher and it wouldn't go all the way back to 15."

I asked, "But why would it be 150? Why not 115?"

Sarah said, "Because the 5 is a 50 already."

"That's an interesting way to look at it," I said. "Since the 5 of the 15 is 50 already, it couldn't be 115. Oh man, this is hard. Keep listening and thinking, Marietta, and I bet it'll become more clear. Why don't you try to continue now, Jesse?"

"Well, 6 and 9 are 15, so that's 150. Then the two 7s are 14, so I'll put the 4 on the 5 and that's 190. Then the 10 from the 14 makes it 200."

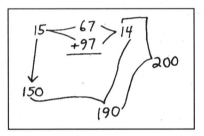

Several children raised their hands. Jesse called on Josh. "I think the 1 in the 14 is a 10 but the. . . ."

Jesse cut him off. "Oh, I got confused. I put the 4 in the wrong place." She paused.

I started to say, "So what's. . . ."

"Wait, wait!" Jesse interrupted.

I beamed. "OK, I'll wait," I said. She was guarding her desire to think this through on her own with such fierce enthusiasm.

After a bit, she said, "I'll put the 10 on the 50 for 60; and then I'll put the 4 on for 164."

A little cheer went up for Jesse.

Wondering together:
How did you get that?
What are you going through?

In this discussion, the children did two hard things which seem to me to be essential to growth and learning. They said what they were confused about; and when they were confused, they didn't get discouraged and quit, but instead kept struggling to understand. I believe that they can do these difficult things because of two assumptions in these discussions:

• There is no right way to get to the truth. Instead, people have to invent a way to get there.
• Everyone's job is to try to follow everyone else's efforts to get to the truth.

When I think about conversations that have helped me to change, the same two things stand out. When someone wants to know about my experience of a situation and tries to make sense of what I tell her, I become more clear as I grope along in explaining myself. If she then states her own ideas as opinions, I can learn more about what I think from our debate because the assumption is that we both know parts of the truth and can both know more. If, on the other hand, my friend offers her ideas as the truth, my mind clamps shut. For one thing, there is no room to wonder about things if there is already a universal truth. And, also, I feel dumb: there is some global truth which the other takes for granted and to which I haven't been privy. It is very hard to mire about in what is unclear with someone who is so certain. The conversation dead-ends or is filled with pontificating.

In the discussion about the recipe for a tasty Bouly-Swag poison, the assumptions that there are multiple routes to wisdom and that everyone would be trying to understand each other made it safe for Clifford, Marietta, and Jesse to say they didn't understand. Because they were safe, they could muddle about until they got clearer. Clifford became clear through explaining his ideas and Jesse through a combination of explaining and listening. I see this happen every day at math time: children understand by explaining how they are thinking and by debating their differences of opinion. Jesse has thoroughly taken on the idea that she has to be inventing in order to understand: she cuts off Josh in mid-sentence when things start to make sense to her so that she can say it her own way; then later she stops me from talking so that she can have time to figure further herself.

I know how to add 67 and 97 very efficiently but if I had said, "This is how to do this," it would have deadened these children's enthusiasm and made their understanding, if they did gain understanding, far more shallow. Also I would not have known how they were thinking about the problem and therefore how to help them know more. From doing math in this way I have learned to "follow children's thinking instead of leading it" (Duckworth, 1995). I believe that it is my job in both the academic and the social arena to invite children to tell me their thoughts and then try to follow their thinking so that I can help them think further. This is a leap from telling, but a very satisfying leap.

Since I believe that peer interactions are just as important for promoting academic and social growth as teacher/student interactions are, I have tried to find a way that my students can offer each other the same sort of invitation to share, discuss, and debate their thinking. After several tries in math, I have hit on a very productive way for them to do this. Constance Kamii has children say, "I disagree," when one student has a different idea than another. I have never tried this. It seems to me that this response would immediately put a child on the defensive because it emphasizes position-taking rather than inviting an exchange. For a couple of years, I had children say, "Check again," when they disagreed with each other. Eventually I realized that this statement doesn't invite a discussion of opposing views; it just says, "I think you're wrong." I realized, finally, that I could best bring about an interchange of opinions by having the children use the same question that I had come to ask in the group sessions. Since to be productive, the focus has to be on the thinking rather than the answer, I always ask, "*How* are you thinking about this?" instead of *"What* did you come up with?" This question is very non-threatening and when the children use it with each other their work together becomes very productive. If the problem that they are working on is an intriguing one, they naturally want to unravel it; this question— *"How did you get that?"*—focuses them on understanding both their partners' and their own thinking so that they are better able to think through the problem.

I have come to believe that this question lies at the heart of how we can talk with each other in any situation. The philosopher Simone Weil has put it this way, "The only real question to be asked of another is, 'What are you going through?'" (Kazin, 1994, p. 64). To me this question is the same as the one I ask in math. Both questions say, "Your experience and ideas are important to me and by talking about them we can get somewhere." My teaching now revolves around this kind of inquiry and conversation. This is a far cry from the ideas that I began teaching with, ideas that revolved around telling. I first experienced the usefulness and pleasures of this approach in teaching science. When I tried constructivist math techniques I became completely immersed in this way of thinking and it is through immersion in this approach that I have been able to build in myself the faith and patience that make this kind of teaching so satisfying and successful. The pleasure is great in being able to follow a child like Jesse through the labyrinth of her bewilderment toward growing clarity.

FOXES AND FROGS

Creating the real questions:
Where to begin?

Where do I start in trying to create provocative questions? I begin with the belief that children's urge to understand the world is so strong that they will almost always try to puzzle things out if they are presented with situations and questions that are neither beyond them nor beneath them, which neither overwhelm them nor condescend to them. I have found that the best way that I can mine this passion to know is by working to create just the right tension between what the children know and what they don't know. If I can help them become aware of what they already know and then listen very attentively while they are talking about it, I can usually find a place where they will want to find out more.

In January one year, I planned to take my second grade class to a nature center. We were going to explore the woods to try to figure out how animals survive in the winter. A few days before the trip I asked the children what animals they had seen in the winter. They had lots of ideas. Quite a few children that year were especially intrigued by foxes, thanks in part to Roald Dahl's *Fantastic Mr. Fox*, so naturally foxes worked their way into the discussion.

Jenny said, "And foxes eat frogs."

"Will they be able to do this in the winter?" I asked.

Tom answered, "Sure, they can just go down to the stream and catch them."

"But the streams are frozen," Michael said.

"Then where are the frogs?" I asked.

"They must come out before it freezes," Charlie answered.

"Yeah," said Maria, "I've seen frogs sitting on rocks, so I know they can live out of the water."

47

"They must spend the winter out of the ponds," Rocky said.

"I've never seen a frog hopping around in the snow," Jenny countered.

"So they must get frozen in the ice and, like, hibernate there or something," said Michael.

"I go ice fishing with my dad," Tina offered. "We cut holes in the ice and I've never seen any frozen frogs."

"Maybe they make little holes in the ice so they can get out when they need to," said Zelda.

Jack liked this idea. "Then the foxes could wait by the holes. I saw polar bears on TV waiting for seals like that."

The discussion continued but I'll stop there. Because my desire was to make the situation real to the children, I began by asking them about what they already knew—what animals they saw in the winter. This provided the security of the known and made the discussion vividly personal. Starting this way also provided the springboard toward the unknown—but not by itself. I had to stay alert for the place that was likely to hold an intriguing question. I had to squelch my doubts about whether foxes eat frogs even in August and head straight for the problem of whether they could get them in January. I did this because I saw that the juicy question of how the frogs spend the winter lay just around the corner.

About ten years ago I was bothered by this question of what frogs do in the winter myself. If I had told the children what I'd found out about it though, they wouldn't have had this opportunity to grapple with the issue and to understand more clearly the problems and possibilities. I've found that handing out information often deflates learning unless it comes after a debate about the possibilities, just as the thrill of a Hitchcock movie or a Sherlock Holmes story comes from unraveling the clues.

All we had time for that day was to make the situation real and to wonder about the frogs in the winter. But the children's curios-

ity about the difficulties of winter survival and the possible ingenious adaptations had been aroused. They hadn't learned about
what bears and birds and squirrels do in the winter, but they were
intrigued about the dimensions of the problem of winter survival
and they had some new ways to approach thinking about it, so I
felt that I'd done my job. As David Hawkins puts it, "You don't
want to cover a subject; you want to uncover it" (Duckworth, 1987,
p. 7). I believe that the best way to "uncover the subject" is to figure
out what children know and are fascinated by and then to look for
the question that will help them explore what they don't know.

THE ABALONE ARGUMENT

Real questions start with what's known,
even when it's inaccurate.

One year a second grader shared a conch shell that he had found
while vacationing in some sunny place. The sharing sparked a big
response in the other children, so I suggested they could bring in
sea objects that they had found if they wanted. The flood of sea
treasures and the enthusiasm for them that followed led us to a
study of sea life. The discussions about things like clams and
horseshoe crabs were so delightful that I decided to videotape one
of our discussions so that I could share it with other teachers.

The next day's meeting was about an abalone and the discussion lumbered along in an uncharacteristically desultory way. We
talked about the abalone's colors and its holes and barnacles and
then I asked what they wanted to know about it.

Marcus asked, "Why does it have those holes?"

"That's the way it goes to the bathroom," said Julius. He had
read about it in a book.

The conversation was going nowhere. I asked, "Is there any-

49

thing else you want to know about this creature?" No response. Then I said, "Why did I say creature? It doesn't look like a creature. Oh, Julius just said it goes to the bathroom, so it must be a creature."

Ellie raised her hand. "If it was a creature, it would always be attacked because it would have to be like this (she held her hand with the open side up). It couldn't live the other way around because if a creature was in there it would fall out. Anything could easily kill it if it was like this (open side up)."

"Ellie has an interesting point," I said. "She says if it were a creature. . . ."

"It can't be a creature," Ellie interrupted. Then she refuted the going-to-the-bathroom proof of creaturehood. "The holes must happen from the barnacles falling off."

I repeated Ellie's theories about vulnerability and about the barnacles and then asked for ideas about her thoughts.

Ellie's good friend Kalhani said, "It could be a creature because a creature could be connected to the shell like a clam is."

"Could this be, Ellie?" I asked.

"Not really, because how could it be hooked on? There's nothing to hook onto except a little dent."

I asked some children to go to the sea museum we had made and bring over the conch, the horseshoe crab, a murex shell, and a clam shell. I held up the conch shell and the abalone and we studied them for a bit. Then I said about the abalone, "I agree with Ellie that it seems like it would be hard for anything to hold on with all this open space. The conch has a much smaller opening and better places to attach. But what could it be, Ellie, if it weren't a creature?"

"Nothing in it makes it grow," she said. "It isn't like a turtle shell. Things must add on to it and that makes it get bigger. Maybe the barnacles make it grow and when it's fully grown, they fall off. I have one at home that doesn't have any rough spots because it's full grown."

"Smooth on both sides?" I asked.

"Yeah."

Luis said, "I don't think it was ever alive. Maybe it's just the barnacles that go to the bathroom."

I got very excited about this idea. "Luis doesn't believe in Julius's book. He's just like those scientists we talked about yesterday who didn't believe what all the other scientists had been saying about dinoflagellates. He's just like Columbus.

"This is getting to be a mystery. Is it alive? If it is, how could it grow? How could anything hold on to the shell? With this crab and this murex there's a place for the legs and the guts to be on the inside, but not with the abalone. This horseshoe crab that we studied yesterday is shaped like the abalone, and its insides don't fall out." I shook the horseshoe crab. "But it's so much smaller and lighter than the abalone."

Crissy said, "A creature could hang on in the dent."

Ellie refuted this. "If it was hooked on in the dent, it would have to be as small as the dent and it couldn't move this big shell to get food. The shell is too heavy."

There were ten hands in the air now. I called on James. "The creature wouldn't have to be just in the dent. The whole bottom could be filled, like the horseshoe crab. A hook could come out of the body into the dent to hold on. And it could move, even if it was heavy, just by sliming along."

I said, "Yesterday there were lots of different ideas about how the horseshoe crab could move, and now there are different opinions about this. James says it could slime along with part of it holding on in the dent."

Stephen said, "I think it's like a clam. We only have half of it; it has another shell on top. You know how a clam sucks water in and shoots it out? That's how this could move, with all those holes."

"Vroom," I said. "A couple of days ago we learned about the strange way that the conch moves. So maybe this has jet propulsion."

Anna said, "I agree about the two shells, just like a clam, but I think it has legs that come out of the holes."

Ellie wasn't buying any of it. "The holes are too small for legs, and anyway clams don't have legs. And clams don't live in abalone shells. Nothing is supposed to live in it. It's just supposed to be a shell."

Fifteen hands were in the air now. The children all had their own ideas about whether it was a creature and just how it might work if it were. After a bit I stopped the discussion and the children pored over books and magazine articles and called a zoologist at the University of Massachusetts to try to solve the puzzles.

In this discussion, misinformation rather than correct information stimulated the vigor and depth of the inquiry and, ultimately, led to a high level of understanding. Without Ellie's notion that the abalone wasn't a creature at all, we wouldn't have wondered how it could move with such a heavy shell, how it could stay in that shell, how it could stay safe, or what purpose those holes really served. Since I began working in this way I have found that productive discussions often spring from misguided notions. Research has found that two people who begin exchanging incorrect views make more progress more often than pairs in which one person starts with the correct view (Doise and Mugny, 1984, pp 86–87). This book is rooted in the notion that we have to take children's ideas and experiences seriously, no matter how outlandish they may seem, since their ideas and experiences are the only starting points they have for constructing meaning and virtue. Because I have often found "wrong" ideas to be so useful, I always try to be aware of the deadening effect of fact and try to keep my eyes open for an opinion that, whether near the mark or far from it, might connect children to the search for truth—and along the way might connect us to each other.

STUDYING COMMUNITY

The foundation for real questions:
making what's known come alive.

I have said that I can best "uncover" a subject by emphasizing what the children know as they begin. This gives a situation a good chance of becoming vivid enough to stimulate a look into the unknown. Part of my second grade social studies curriculum is the study of community. I had always begun this work by having the children visit and research various community institutions and then create out of unit blocks an operating town based on what they had learned. Though this had produced adequate work, one year I decided to see what would happen if I started the study by having the children build the institutions and businesses first, get the town going, and then deal with whatever problems arose from their imperfect creations. The results were thrilling.

• When business slowed down at the pizza parlor, the owners visited a local pizza establishment and found out about advertising, about offering more variety on their menu, about specials, and about how remodeling might help provide some fresh appeal.
• The clothing store had the opposite problem. Since we were using trolls for the people in the town and all the trolls needed clothes, the store sold its entire inventory in one day. The owners brought some very real questions about supply and demand to local retailers.
• Before the businesses even opened, the question of money sup-

ply reared its head. How did people get money anyway? From the bank. But how did the money get in the bank? Gradually the idea surfaced that the bank didn't just give money away, but rather got it from people who earned it and chose to keep it in the bank. It became clear that these people got paid by their employers. But where did the employers get the money to buy the things that they would sell? They must borrow money from the bank. But where does the bank get all that money from? They just make it at a mint!? But then what would be a fair way for the mint to distribute the money? All these hitherto unthought of questions became very alive because they arose from the real needs of the town.

- The bus company had very few riders. Little by little the proprietors discovered things like routes and schedules and promotions.
- The children's section of the hospital became very noisy once injured troll children began feeling better. The hospital staff lengthened visiting hours, made sure there were more activities for the children in their rooms, and hired a part-time social worker.
- Money disappeared from a hotel room. There was an accusation of burglary—but there was no court system, not even any police. These institutions were brought on board. Children whose trolls sold clothes and cut hair had them take on second careers as lawyers during the burglary trial. They consulted real lawyers about the rules governing testimony and evidence. They saw the presumption of innocence as a particularly strange way of doing things. (The trial ended in a hung jury.)

This work was far more vital than what I had done in previous years and I believe the reason was because a creative tension was established by having children start with what they knew and letting the problems grow from there. We can only take in information for which we have a frame of reference. In my old way of doing this work, where children did the research before building and living in the town, their frame of reference was very limited. In this new way of working, where the research was based on the problems that arose from trying to run a service or business, the children's frame of reference took on new dimensions and they were very motivated to find solutions.

My job while the town was operating was the same as in the winter survival discussion. I had to be able to follow the children's thinking and to be on the look out for the question that would most likely "uncover" more understanding for them. Sometimes— with the bus company, the hospital, and the money supply question—I helped them to think more about the problem. Other times I helped them think about how they could find the information that they wanted.

Early in this study of community, the need to make some choices about the town always arises. How will money be distributed? Can trolls from home be used in the town? What will the transportation system be? Zoning issues arise about the size and quantity of buildings. The question which I lay before the children is, "How will all these decisions be made?" The possibilities that they come up with usually range from consensus through anarchy and include various forms of democracy and autocracy. One year a group was trying to decide between monarchy, representative democracy, and direct democracy.

"I think we should elect three people to decide things," Michael said.

"Why?" I asked.

"It would be easier than everyone always voting. We would trust them to decide things." Michael liked things to be easy.

Sally spoke next. "I think the representative way would be best, too, because we wouldn't take up all our time with discussions."

I said, "The staff of our school thought what you thought, Sally. We used to have all of us make decisions but we got tired of it. So now we have a few people do it. The trouble is that a lot of us complain because we don't have enough say in things."

Maurice said, "If only three people decide things, it may not be fair to some people."

"And it would be worse if there was a queen," said Kate. "She could make a decision that wouldn't work and it would be permanent and then our town wouldn't work forever."

"Can anyone think of a way around that problem?" I asked.

"Vote for the king," said Marietta.

"Then you could depose him by voting, too," I said, getting in some fancy language.

"Yeah," Sarah offered, "but then I'd feel bad. I'd say, 'Why did I vote for him?' We should trust a king if we elect him, but we wouldn't when things go wrong."

"Sounds hard," I said. "Do you think we'd have people running around saying, 'Off with his head?'"

"Yeah." "Nah." Giggling.

Adam spoke next. "I think everyone has to vote about the problems that come up because if it's just a few people, they'll favor their friends."

"Happens all the time," I said. "It's called political favors. But if you choose pure democracy you have to be willing to sit down and make all these decisions."

"I like both kinds of democracy," Abbey said. "It would be better for everybody to vote, but it would take too much time from playing in the town."

"There, Abbey," I said, "you have defined this nasty problem exactly."

"I have a solution," said Kim. "Why don't we just vote on things without talking about them?"

"No advertising on TV," I said, "no campaign promises, no discussion. Just voting."

Jon said, "Three kids could decide things faster and there are some smart kids in this class that would know what to do about things."

Jeremy challenged his best buddy, Jon. "I have a question for the people who are for the representative way. Why are you in such a hurry to get things over with?"

"Because it'll be faster and give us more troll time," said Josh.

Jerry countered this argument. "If a few people are deciding, it could take *more* time, because if they didn't agree they would argue and there wouldn't be any new ideas and the decision might never get made."

"OK," I said. "Take a moment to think about which way you want to vote. Remember that all the other decisions depend on this one."

The results of the secret ballot were: monarchy = 0; couldn't decide = 4; representative democracy = 5; direct democracy = 14.

This outcome was quite remarkable to me. This group of children was so invested in figuring out problems and in having a say in how things would run that they were willing to give up play time in their town to do so, even knowing that they would have to stop their play to discuss quite frequently. For them to have made a choice like this is a clear sign that they derived a great deal of satisfaction from puzzling through problems and taking responsibility.

CHAPTER 4

Getting on

Their Side

They tattle and whine,
they don't do their homework,
they hit each other.
How am I supposed to
ally with these children?

I RECENTLY UNDERWENT A MINOR OPERATION. THE HOS-pital staff urged me to get out of bed and walk as soon as possible. Before I went to sleep at night, the nurse said that I might start to feel better during the night and that if I did I should try to get up and walk a bit. After she left, I raised myself up onto my elbows. This took me several minutes and was very painful. I decided that getting up would have to wait until morning.

In the middle of the night, however, I woke up with the very clear idea that in order to get better I had to get out of bed. So I spent ten minutes fighting the piercing pain and, inch by inch, I raised myself to a standing position. Then the pain and the weirdness of being vertical took over and I collapsed into a lump on the floor, pulling my IV pole on top of me. The crashing brought a large number of helpers scurrying into the room.

Through my pain, confusion, and growing nausea, I heard a tense male voice giving orders from a far corner of the room. A nurse roughly tried to transfer me onto a stretcher, angry that I wasn't doing it right. Another nurse silently pushed at me; yet another fidgeted with the stretcher, bored. Then a different nurse knelt next to me on the floor. She bent over and held me. The other nurses blurred. She asked me if I felt nauseated and then reassured me that I was going to be fine. I wasn't at all sure that she was right, but I felt soothed by her warmth and confidence.

The next day I felt privileged to have had this tiny surreal experience. I had had a rare close-up reminder of what it is like to be a child: I had been extremely vulnerable and at the mercy of those in power. I was struck by how precisely and dramatically the emotions of each care-giver resounded within me. Without the

59

armor of my adult reasoning and defenses, I felt powerfully every nuance of resentment, anxiety, confusion, distancing, and warmth that came my way. This brief return to a child's reality made vivid for me the chasm between me and the children whom I teach.

The vulnerability that I experienced is only one aspect of the huge difference between us. The children have unbounded energy and I'm usually tired by noon. We clash in values, style, and personality. Race and culture often separate us. I'd like Emma to wait her turn to talk, but she'd rather say what she's thinking as soon as it crosses her mind. I wish that Eli would share the calculator with Frankie so they could get on with their math, but he's hiding it from him because of some grudge left over from recess. I wish that Aliesha would see how intriguing her reading homework is, but she's much more involved figuring out intriguing excuses for not doing it.

I've come to feel that my first job in teaching, the one from which everything else derives, is to become like the nurse who was able to reach across the chasm separating her experience from mine; instead of turning from my misery, she saw what I needed, asked me about it, and did what she could to help. She allied with me. This chapter is about my attempts to become like her in my teaching, to bridge the gap between the children and myself.

LAYING THE FOUNDATION

When I was lying on the floor in the hospital only one of the five nurses responded with empathy and with an attempt to comfort me. My collapse was annoying to some of the nurses and seemed downright obnoxious to others. The problem that I run into with my central task of allying with children is the same problem that most of those nurses had—there is so much in children's behavior that seems annoying and obnoxious to me.

They tease, tattle, whine, blame, lie, forget homework, hit each other, lose books, stand on furniture, throw food, refuse to work, put themselves down, hide each other's lunches, brag, run around the classroom, refuse to stand up for themselves, snatch each other's things, call each other names, talk ceaselessly at a quiet time, booby trap desks, deface work, trip, bully. . . . The list could go on. The question is, how can I get myself to ally with children when they do these things? I will tell two stories that hold the germ of an answer for me.

Barbara, a teacher of seven-year-olds, had a clever idea for a parent night: all the children would make simple dummies of themselves and seat them at their desks. When the parents came into the room that night, they could locate their child's work by finding their "child." The day before the parents' night, the children cut out oak tag hands and were coloring them, trying to get their skin shades right by blending crayons. Except for Hank: he had made his hands green.

When Barbara saw this, she was upset. She thought of how often Hank was extremely silly at meetings and of how impulsive he was. Now green hands! Barbara walked over to him, irritated.

"Hank, why did you make your hands green?"

Hank hesitated, looking at the hands. "I don't know."

"What will your parents think when they come in and see that you've made your hands green?"

"I . . . I couldn't find the right shade."

Barbara talked to Hank about silliness and then worked with him to find and blend the colors that would match his skin. Then it was time for lunch. Hank would redo the hands in the afternoon.

Hank diligently got to work right after lunch. Barbara glanced over to see how he was doing. She couldn't believe her eyes—he was making the hands green again! To keep from boiling over, Barbara went to the door and signaled to Sue, the first grade teacher in the room across the hall. Sue saw that Barbara was upset and came over to her. Barbara told what had happened and then said, "I've had it with this need to be ridiculous all the time. What do you think I should do?"

Sue, who had been Hank's first grade teacher, said that this time the answer was simple. Hank was color blind. Although this tale seems to have a trick ending, the conclusion has a lesson for me about searching for causes behind offensive behavior.

I found myself in a similar situation a few years ago. I couldn't for the life of me establish a decent relationship with a girl in my class named Bridget. She drove me crazy. She defied all rules, moped when called to task, undermined other children at every opportunity, and only did the work that she wanted to do. For the previous two years she had been taught by a very loving teacher who, when I described the problems that I was having, confided to me that Bridget was the first child in her twenty years of teaching whom she had been unable to like. This solidified my growing suspicion that the situation was hopeless and I began actively to dislike Bridget.

In mid-winter I had a meeting with her psychologist who told me that Bridget demonstrated many of the characteristics of a type of Attention Deficit Disorder, ADD. Although I had taught many ADD children, I had never thought of Bridget in this light. This notion completely altered my attitude toward her. I changed my approach with Bridget, her behavior began to change in small but important ways, and by the end of the year we had become quite fond of each other.

I am not saying that we should suspect organic disability at every turn. What these stories make me wonder is why I often need such obvious physical disorders to move me to try harder to understand, to make allowances, to try to get on the side of a child. I have too often viewed emotional and learning problems

as matters of will; I've thought that children were somehow resolutely choosing to undermine their own best interests. But I am
often blind to my own flaws and I find it hard to change even
when I become aware of them. I usually need someone who can
help me see what needs might be behind my foolish behaviors and
what better ways I might have to meet those needs. I want to be
that someone for the children I teach.

My thinking about this was defined wonderfully for me by
something I read by Janet Preston, a social worker at a school in
Seattle: "When you love people, you overlook their faults and you
address their needs" (Paraskevas, 1993, p. 20). Adopting this attitude does not mean that I coddle children or honor their excuses.
Often enough what a child needs is to be stretched. But since being so blind about Bridget's needs, I try harder to search annoying behavior for the need that it betrays and search for the resources in the child that will help her meet that need. The stories
about Hank and Bridget urge me to hunt down the good in children. When they behave badly or have trouble learning, I try to
apply the same perspective that I have for physical handicaps: I
try to look beyond the flaws to the child's needs and the goodness,
so that I can get on the child's side.

I will give an example of this effort in a situation where organic disability played no part. Once again, the story comes from
lunch time. The lunch teacher, Ms. Jacobs, had been telling me
that Melissa frequently had some woe to report to her about Nick.
I could imagine it—Nick could be quite a pest. On the other hand,
Melissa loved to play the victim. Ms. Jacobs said that she had taken
the tack of telling Melissa to go back and stand up for herself.

One day Ms. Jacobs was sick and I had responsibility for
lunch time. Melissa, Tamala, and Monique had to join Nick and
Charlie at a table because all of the other tables were taken. Pass-
ing by, I heard Monique tell the boys, "You can't sit across from

each other. You have to sit next to each other." Because the boys were sitting across from each other, one of the girls would have to sit separated from the others. Monique's comment, besides being untrue and bossy, had a very snotty tone.

Ignoring everything but my own pique at this three-headed insult, I said, "That's ridiculous, Monique. Of course they can sit across from each other." They sat down, Tamala separated from her friends.

Moments later the trio of girls popped out of their chairs and came running over to me. "Nick called us slobs," Melissa said, horrified.

I went back with them to the table. "You called them slobs?" I asked Nick.

"Well, Melissa teased me," he answered.

"As soon as we sat down," Melissa countered, "Nick said, 'I know what we'll do. We just won't talk to them.'"

Charlie said, "And then Melissa says, 'We just won't talk to them,'" mimicking the mimicking in singsong.

So then Nick called the girls slobs. Here was a nice little nightmare—blaming, slander, exclusivity, righteousness, and revenge all built on a healthy foundation of previously unresolved quarrels. No wonder it burst into flames in seconds, especially with the gasoline of judgment tossed on it by the teacher.

"You can continue eating," I said, "once we figure out how this could work better."

"Well, they could eat over on the rug," Charlie said.

"Yeah, they could eat over on the rug," Tamala said.

A great start.

"Please talk about what *you'll* do to help the situation," I said.

"We could just not talk to them," Nick said.

"You could do that," I said. "Can you think of anything else that might help?"

At this point Zelda, who had come late to lunch, joined the table. Nick said, "We'll talk to Zelda."

"Any other possibilities?" I asked.

There was a long pause. Then Melissa said, "We could talk about something we won't fight about."

"Like what?" I asked.

"Halloween," Nick suggested.

Charlie and Melissa said, "Yeah!" at the same time.

I left them all to a very animated conversation. Nick and Melissa were especially chatty with each other.

At the start of this story, my brusqueness and judgment and preconceptions, my avoidance of dealing thoughtfully with a hard situation, made a bad scene worse. Then I changed: I set aside both my whiners-be-damned and my Nick-as-provocateur typecasting so that I could do the work of entering the fray. The situation was a tremendous mess. Although this was a battle in a long-running war, and although the combatants' positions were deeply embedded in their personal weaknesses, and although I myself had shown them that prejudice and cynicism were to be the order of the day, I then came back believing that things could be better. I believed that these children could work things out with each other if they could just be held to the task.

When I look back at what I actually did in that conversation, it seems very unsophisticated. I exercised some patience and did a little bit of limit-setting, but mostly what I did was display some raw faith. This kind of believing lies at the heart of my effort to ally with children—and thus at the heart of my teaching. Therefore, one of my most essential tasks is to construct and then to nurture this faith within myself. Learning to get on a child's side when it's hard to do was the first and most important step that I had to make in order to become a better teacher. As a forty-year-old with a strong foundation in cynicism, I was fortunate enough to begin working in a school with extraordinarily positive teachers. During this time I was also working on changes in my personal life that allowed me to believe more in myself and in others. Then I stumbled onto the writings of Vivian Paley (1981, 1984, 1990, 1992). Her profound belief in the potential for good in every individual further inspired me. Though this is not a self-help book about personal growth, I do feel that in order to teach well I had to be receptive to outside sources of inspiration about the goodness of people and about our ability to change for the better, and also to work to find the sources of that inspiration within myself.

These internal changes are not the only source of my growing ability to believe in children. I am helped equally in this effort by using the tools that I have collected over the years to spur me to ally with children when their behavior is getting under my skin. Just as my belief encourages me to ally with children, these practical steps that I take to get on a child's side stimulate my belief in them. These tools fall into two categories: understanding the children and understanding myself.

UNDERSTANDING CHILDREN— WHAT'S GOING ON FOR THEM?

In order to ally with a child who is being mean or stubborn or who can't learn to read, it is essential to believe that things can get better. My allying will be hollow, however, if I don't understand the child as well as believe in her. I have five techniques that help me understand children so that I can ally with them.

The first thing that I always do to try to get myself beyond my irritation when a child is being rude or sneaky or aggressive or manipulative is to wonder why the annoying behavior might be happening so that I can develop a productive way of relating to the child around the issue. This perhaps seems an obvious step, but I have too often skipped it. I'll think, *How can Luis possibly be so bossy?* and *How can I stop him?* instead of *Why is he doing that?* I find that looking at the possible sources of offensive behaviors makes my thinking about a child more flexible and also starts to link me to her. It moves me from a feeling of being besieged toward a sense that we have something to work on together. So when behavior bugs me I have now developed the habit of asking, *What's making her do this?* or *How does it serve her?* These bedrock empathic questions can then lead me to reach out with conversation or with action.

I remember the very first time that I was able to use this simple but powerful technique. Many years ago I taught a second grade girl named Joan who had no friends. This was not surprising since she spent all of her social energy trying to relate to her teacher. The trouble was that her teacher didn't like her. From my relationship with Joan I was learning one of my teaching weaknesses: an aversion to cloyingly dependent children. With every picture she painted for me, I liked her less.

In the winter my supervisor asked me what I could do to make things better. The question surprised me. I had thought that Joan was the one who was supposed to do the changing. How was I supposed to like someone who asked me to fuss over her dress every morning? Her neediness and my annoyance with it had reached a plateau for a while, but was just starting to escalate again. *Why is she more needy now?* I asked myself. *What change has there been?* Then it occurred to me: because she was a very gifted reader she had started to leave the room during language arts in order to work with a third grade reading group. Reading groups were the heart of this classroom. So much revolved around the stories that we read and the projects that came from them. For the first time all year I felt bad for Joan—she was missing all this fun.

I decided that she should come back to our room at reading time, that she should join a lower level group so she could write vocabulary words onto construction paper pieces of eight and hide them with us on our classroom island. I also decided that I would work with her once a week on reading at her higher level. This combination of including her in a reading group and my giving her attention for something she was skilled at took a big bite out of her dependency and out of my distaste for her.

I believe that this change came about because my supervisor asked me to take some responsibility for the problem. The first step in my doing that was to wonder what could be going on for Joan, why her neediness had escalated. Now when a child is frustrating me, either in an academic or social area, I try as often as I can to make a search for causes be the first step I take in trying to help things improve.

The teacher as student

I have found that one of the most powerful levers for helping me understand and then ally with a difficult child is to study her. I tell my classes that one of my jobs as their teacher is to know them well and that sometimes I can do that best if I can watch them without interruption. So when I put on my baseball hat, I am invisible. Several times a week I observe a child or a group of children; I record what I see and hear, writing furiously for five to fifteen minutes, trying to get down every word, gesture, and facial expression. I write down only what I observe, no voice-overs or analysis. Sometimes I use a tape recorder and then listen later. I find out a tremendous amount in reading over or listening to these observations and, as often as not, much of it comes as a surprise to me.

This happened one September when I did a written observation of a boy whose reputation had preceded him to second grade. It was reported that he had no friends and that the reason for this was that he ignored his classmates' desires. But when I put on my hat and observed him during an art period where the children were making three dimensional houses, I saw him create beautiful furniture and give it to other children; and I saw the other children repeatedly ignore him when he asked for the scissors or tried to begin a conversation.

Besides gaining invaluable data and understanding, I have experienced another, unexpected benefit from these observations. This effort to watch and listen to a child so closely almost always moves me to care more about them and their struggles, just from the sheer intimacy of the effort. From these observations I gain information to mull over and grist for future conversations, but I also experience an immediate gain in connection.

The teacher as Sherlock Holmes—Staying alert for clues

Another way to get on the side of a child who is annoying me is to stay alert for ways that the child might reveal other sides of herself. I recently taught a girl named Sally who was very unpopular with her classmates. She taunted, teased, undermined, blamed, and frequently talked about disgusting things at the lunch table. And she would never admit to her role in conflicts.

I had been avoiding Sally all fall. She seemed so dedicated to her destructive behaviors that I hadn't been able to summon the energy that I knew would be required to understand what was going on inside her, much less to help her change what she was doing. Her absolute denial of ever doing any wrong particularly galled and intimidated me.

I sometimes do a scaled sociogram with my classes—the children confidentially give a number rating to how much they like each other. I had done this with this class. Sally's average was the lowest in the class. The children also rated what they thought their own average would be. The highest possible score was ten and Sally gave herself a 9.9.

I told another teacher who knew Sally well that she had done this. "I would have expected she would do that," he said. "She's in a world of her own. What hope is there with that attitude?"

But Sally's fantasy about how much her classmates liked her started me thinking differently about her and it activated my empathy for her. The same girl who needed to be so nasty and to undermine her classmates also needed to pretend that she hadn't ever done *any* of that. It occurred to me that the principle that the best defense was a good offense might be at work here. Maybe she could only feel all right by telling herself this huge lie so that she wouldn't let in the other possibilities. Now I had to know what pain was driving her to such extremes.

My own and my fellow teacher's stereotyping of Sally had been our way of avoiding the discomfort of looking at, worrying over, and becoming involved with her pain. Once I was able to be open to Sally's showing me another side of herself, I began to get on her side—which led to some dramatic changes for her.

Collegiality—possibilities and perils

A conversation with a colleague is often very useful in freeing up my thinking when I am stuck about how to proceed with a difficult child. Sometimes my peers offer a valuable perspective that I hadn't considered. Sometimes just the chance to say things out loud helps me become clearer.

As with observation, just talking about a child often helps me feel more connection to her, but it can have the opposite effect if I am not careful. Becoming allied with a child calls on both my mind and my will. I have to increase not only my understanding about a child but also my desire to improve our connection. This means that I have to use care in getting help from peers. Venting about a child can open a door for me, but it is very easy to stay stuck in the venting phase, with my colleague and me reinforcing each other's stereotypes. Unless I keep the goal of connection before me, these conversations can merely move from venting to whining.

Don't forget to have fun

I come to know children not only from thinking about and discussing their bad behavior and circuitous thinking. One of the most powerful ways to understand and ally with children is to appreciate, encourage, and enjoy them. Children know that I am on their side not only when I delve into their upsets with them, but also when I have fun with them.

I was once confronted by a sixth grade girl who didn't like something I had done. We had an initial discussion and planned a time when we would continue. During the couple of days before our second meeting, I worked with her on a research paper about D-Day. She was writing about the mix of bravery and fear in soldiers. I thought her topic was very original and that the way she was writing about it was ingenious. I let her know this. I asked her what she was afraid of. "Heights," she answered. At recess I helped her walk across the top row of the outdoor bleachers.

When we met to talk the second time about our conflict, she said that since the day she'd confronted me she'd realized what a good teacher I was. She said that she now realized that she'd challenged me because she was mad at me about something completely different that had happened a month before. I believe that because I had appreciated her writing and we had been able to enjoy each other's company, she came to see that I was on her side.

I try to build into my day lots of opportunities to appreciate and enjoy my students. I discovered my best method for doing this many years before I was able to put it into practice. One morning ten years ago while I was on a break, I dropped by a second grade classroom. The *Nutcracker* was on the phonograph, the children were building and acting and painting, and there was the teacher, Jay Lord, sitting in a rocking chair, watching the room, hearing the tales children would bring him, calling a girl over to chat about something he had seen. I thought, *I'm doing it all wrong; this is the way to teach.* But I didn't have a clue of how to get to that state.

Seven years later I was giving a workshop for teachers. While we were discussing how children come to trust adults, the image of Jay's paradise jumped back into my head. The next week I got a comfortable chair. I put it in the middle of my classroom and started sitting there for the first fifteen minutes of school each day. Suddenly there was time to tell David how great his bright new African hat looked next to his black skin, to notice that Brian gave Nick a wind-up car when he came in, to hear about Melanie's new baby chickens, and to see why Patty never finished her morning spelling work. Now I could have those conversations that had gotten lost in the hurly-burly of yesterday.

"Jacob, I was amazed that you didn't get frustrated when you couldn't figure out how to build that Lego robot yesterday."

"Rocky, Angela told me that she would like me to help the two of you talk about the trouble that you had working together at math yesterday."

Now I could help Daren work on making his entry into school in the mornings a little less like a rocket landing. Now I was sure to have a tiny chat with every child when they first came in, to hear about Zelda's nightmare and Gabe's riddle, to see

Nora's sketchbook and Jacob's snakeskin. We started our days now connecting about our lives, about struggles and triumphs, about bikes and necklaces.

What did I need to understand before I could put into practice what I had seen Jay doing seven years before? I needed to find out that appreciating, encouraging, and enjoying are the bedrock connections that let me understand the children and let them trust me. I needed to come to believe that clearing out fifteen minutes of my morning for this purpose would be worthwhile in the long run.

The easy chair has turned out to be a terrific tool for helping me know and enjoy my students. Another way that especially helps me is to give my students every opportunity to do what they do best so that I can appreciate and enjoy their skills and accomplishments. Working with Joan in an area where she was an expert was an important part of what turned things around with her. I begin every school year with several days devoted to the children sharing something they are particularly skilled at doing. Children ride bikes, play violin, take care of their younger brothers, and make bird nests out of mud and grass. I find it especially important to give children the chance to succeed in physical undertakings. It is for this reason that I put a lot of energy every fall into teaching soccer. Though I am not a skilled art teacher, I try to be sure that these skills don't get relegated to "specials," that there are plenty of opportunities for children to express themselves artistically in my room so that I'll be able to know and enjoy this side of them.

IT TAKES TWO TO TANGO— WHAT'S GOING ON FOR ME?

In my effort to ally, I have to work not only to understand what's going on for the children. I also have to know what I am bringing to the dynamic.

How am I like this annoying child?

It helps me get out of ruts with children to be able to figure out which personalities rub me the wrong way. Joan taught me that the mousy, dependent child is very hard for me; I know that I'm going to have to make extra efforts with these children. I also know that dishonesty especially rankles me, so I've had to work on my knee-jerk reactions to it. In fact I have quite a few pet peeves. I am easily put off by children who brag or whine and those who are controlling or act entitled. If I don't notice that these things are operating for me, I usually wind up in a power struggle with these children. John Nicholls described this state eloquently in a book he wrote about (and with) a wonderful teacher, Sue Hazzard (1993). The book is full of examples of Sue's "ingenuity, wit, and goodwill" (p. 57). However, during several weeks of conflict with a boy who consistently got her goat, these qualities deserted Sue. Nicholls describes the result in this way.

> It is easy, when teaching, to find oneself doing things one had no intention of doing—things that make one feel ridiculous, less than adult. Teachers can become as silly as seven-year-olds battling to sit by the window in the family car. Everyone in such situations becomes less than themselves. (P. 58)

I have found that one of the best ways to avoid these power struggles is to ask myself in what ways I have the trait that is bothering me. In what situations do I talk out during meetings? When do I shirk work? How do I put people down? Don't I sometimes exaggerate my accomplishments? Why? What makes me grouchy? I've found that if I hunt a little, I can almost always find a situation when I do the same things that are bothering me. Doing this helps me in several ways. I gain some insight into what might be motivating the child; and finding that a child and I have the same weakness takes the edge off my irritation, creates a connection to her, and gives me some ideas about how to talk about the problem with her in a nonjudgmental way.

Monitoring myself—listening in

Neither my life in school nor my life away from school is particularly blissful and smooth for very long. My car breaks down, I quarrel with my friends, I get sick, and I worry about my children. I have to keep a watch on my moods, needs, biases, weaknesses, and limits in order to see how they are affecting my work. If I can monitor how my emotions are at play in my classroom, I can better put a brake on them when they are destructive and better allow my joyful, level, and nurturant sides to dominate.

One of the best ways to do this self-monitoring is simply to listen to myself, to what I am saying and how I am saying it. What's going on for me leaks out in the way that I talk. I know what I sound like when I'm happy, relaxed, curious, flexible, enthusiastic, sincere, playful, or patient. I know the difference when I sound tense, short, angry, controlling, hurried, sarcastic, manipulative, or harsh. As I teach, I try to listen to myself and when I hear the harsh, stiff, or rushed tone or words creeping in, I take note and try to figure out why I am talking that way. Sometimes just listening to the words that come out of my mouth is enough to turn me around.

WHY MAKE A HUGE JOB EVEN LARGER?

In this book I am urging us to get on the side of all the children that we teach—especially the most difficult ones. To do this would seem to make our already huge job even larger. Teaching academics for the elementary school teacher can now include reading, writing, and math (all to be done in new and better ways), science (natural and physical), social studies (including history, geography, and government), spelling, grammar, health (along with personal safety and drug prevention), computer literacy, art, and more. We have children with special needs who need mainstreaming, parents who need conferences, reports to write (in narrative please), behavior plans to monitor, homework to correct, and we'd better make sure our rooms are clean, safe, and beautiful as well. We are expected to foster children's initiative, responsibility, fairness, problem solving capabilities, creativity, enthusiasm, kindness, assertiveness, and persistence, as well as their ability to process complex matters rationally and discuss them thoroughly. Teachers are urged to be structured but not rigid, to know when to push and when to let up, to keep their sense of humor, to admit mistakes, to appreciate, to encourage, and to enjoy.

Why add something else to this already bulging list? I believe that attempting to understand how children think and what motivates them and then working to ally with them does add to the job, but that it can also make it easier and more satisfying. I'll explain what I mean.

One year I was in charge of recess during the month of September. Every day two third graders would tell me that some classmates were bothering them. Daily I told them, "Don't tattle. Go play." Late that October I ate with Mrs. LaBelle, who had been on recess duty that month. "How are the tattlers?" I asked.

She looked blankly at me for a moment and then said, "Oh, you mean Jason and Sue?"

"Right."

"They did report about some children bothering them at the start of the month, but they don't do it anymore."

"I'm very impressed," I said. "What did you do?"

Mrs. LaBelle looked puzzled. "I listened to their complaints and talked with them about what they thought," she said.

Now I was puzzled. "Were the problems legitimate?" I asked. "Sometimes they were, sometimes they weren't," she answered.

Mrs. LaBelle looked beyond these children's complaining, respecting that they might have a real need. She merely listened and talked. Why hadn't I thought of doing something so simple? I didn't think of it because I had the children safely tucked away as tattlers. If, instead of dismissing the children, I had opened up a discussion with them, I would have put myself in for some extra work and some turmoil; I would have had to sort through the stories I heard, rethink my perspective, steal a couple of minutes from time that might be spent in a more leisurely fashion, and enter more fully into the dark muddle of human motivation. The other way was easier—in the short run anyway. I find that there is more satisfaction in working to empathize, but as with most crafts—sewing and carpentry come to mind—I have to take into account the trade-off between the amount of labor and the amount of satisfaction.

I taught a boy named Sam a few years ago who kept knocking over other children's block buildings. At first I employed various restrictions—with no effect. Sam and I had a decent bond and eventually I got him to stop knocking down buildings because of this—for me, as it were. But I never thought much about what he was getting at by being so destructive nor did I muck around with him about what might be going on. That seemed like too much work. Now I see him, a much older boy, sabotaging other children's erector set constructions. I had been able to gain greater peace in our room when I was his teacher, but I hadn't done the work that might have helped Sam take more charge of his antisocial side.

I recently had a similar experience that had a better ending. A few years ago, I taught a boy named Mickey in second grade.

He loved to bug other children—poking them in the ribs, hiding their things. When I would address him about one of these mini-attacks, he wouldn't say a word but would move his face from theatrical shock to ugly disgust: to think that I could imagine that he might be to blame! I could never get much beyond my revulsion at his surliness and wasn't much help to him.

Three years later I had the chance to teach Mickey again in fifth grade. Early in September, while I was monitoring lunch, I saw him dump some juice on another child. I said to the teacher with whom I was standing, "I don't want to deal with this stuff again." As I walked towards him, I felt my disbelief growing that this regressed behavior was still his mode. I took him aside. Then as I sat down to talk with him, I felt the failures of my past work with him staring coldly at me and I knew that I had to try something new. I was silent for a few moments trying to think of what that might be.

Finally I said, "I wonder why you bug other kids. I know that I can be annoying when I'm mad about something. Is that the same for you?"

"No." But no ugly look of disgust.

"Some people that I know bug to get attention."

"Not me."

"Maybe you just like to."

"Yeah, it's fun."

Sure, he wanted to get me off his back. But because I had started with wondering what was going on for him instead of accusing him, because I allied with him by admitting that I can be annoying and angry, he was able to stay away from his glaring denials and a door had been opened which led to several months of discussion about his urge to annoy. In one way my discussions with Mickey made more work for me, but avoiding this power struggle also made my job easier.

A final word about the techniques that I have spoken about in this chapter. Over the years I have given many workshops for teachers and have passed on what I feel are valuable techniques and methods. In sports and music, good technique is important, and teaching is no different. Where do I put my feet for a backhand in tennis; how do I hold the flute; when do I ask a question about the dragonfly and when do I give some information? Too often, though, when I put a good technique or system into practice I expect the technique or system to do the job. The trouble with this is that the techniques I use won't work unless I have understood their spirit and made the spirit my own. I mentioned earlier a school that I visited with some colleagues. Though I had passed on many useful techniques to the teachers at that school, it was clear that I had failed to communicate the *spirit* of what I believe about teaching. As I teach I continually have to check the methods that I use to see if they are helping me get to the spirit of my principles. When I have failed to do this, I have presided over stale meetings, taught math lessons that went nowhere, and promoted kindness that had little chance of being heartfelt. Sitting in that easy chair every morning doesn't guarantee that I am becoming allied with children. I *will* be allied with them if I believe that they can learn and can behave well, even when this is far from evident, and if I try to understand why they are having such a hard time doing those things.

CHAPTER 5

Four Stories About

Responsibility

and Judgment

THE ULTIMATE GOAL OF MY TEACHING IS TO HELP CHIL-
dren learn to create their own solutions to the problems of learning and living ethically. Sharing responsibility with them and being non-judgmental undergird all my efforts to achieve this goal.

THE STARING MACHINE

When children in my classes are working individually or in groups
and I need to get everyone's attention (for an announcement or
perhaps to get input from them about something), I ring a bell. I
work to make these exchanges and announcements succinct and
interesting and from early in the year I help the children learn to
meet my expectation that they will give their full attention during these "freezes." By October most children see the reasons for
being attentive during a freeze and they listen and participate well.
But every year a handful find it hard to do, usually the fidgety
ones, but also those who would rather continue what they are doing than listen to a teacher or contribute to the group. Years ago
I adopted a very efficient technique for getting those in the second category to freeze. I would tell them that when I saw that
they needed help paying attention during a freeze, I would give
them a signal to come stand next to me. I found that children
hated doing this and almost universally chose to become attentive when the bell rang if this were the alternative.

One year I had two highly creative second graders who always
continued with their creativity after the bell rang. After one such
"working freeze" during October I went over to these two girls,
preparing my usual spiel. At this point in my teaching, however,

I had become disenchanted with external control techniques and was experimenting with real questions, so when I opened my mouth something new came out.

"What are you doing, Kathleen?" I asked.

"Drawing the princess for that story I'm writing about Uglytown."

"I like those warts on her nose," I said. "What are you up to, Julia?"

"I'm making earrings for my stuffed tiger."

"Very clever," I said. "Both of you please put your things down for a minute so we can chat." They did this. "You two have so many great ideas, like this princess's nose and these earrings. The group could use some of your great ideas. But we never get to hear any of them during freezes because you both keep working. I wonder what makes it so hard for some kids to stop working?"

"You're just so tempted," said Julia, "because you really want to do your ideas."

"Yeah," Kathleen echoed. "You think your idea is so great so you're really, really tempted to keep doing it."

"Does this ever happen to me?" I wondered aloud. "Oh, sure. Sometimes I get up really early to write stories. It's one of the things I really like to do. Most of the time I'm so into it that I don't stop for breakfast—sometimes I don't even stop for lunch. So I know what you mean. Do you know what I mean when I say that the group could use your ideas?"

They mumbled that they knew.

"What do you think would help you listen and give your ideas?"

"I don't know," Julia said. They both looked down at their shoes. I let my question hang in the air. Finally Julia looked up with a twinkle in her eye and said, "Maybe it would help if I just stared at you and didn't look down at my things." She demonstrated, giving me a big bug-eyed stare. This may sound as if it were hostile, but it was sincere. Julia had a penchant for the dramatic.

I chuckled and asked Kathleen if she thought that would help. She mumbled that it might.

"The staring machine," I said. "We could try it. Do you want me to say 'Staring machine' when I ring the bell so that you can remember or do you want to try it without the reminder?" They both wanted to try it without a reminder. From that point on, Julia participated more fully in freezes. After a few days she didn't need the crutch of staring and gave it up. Kathleen needed more work on the issue. Julia backslid a little in the late winter, but a booster conversation helped her get back on track.

Avoiding blame

I wanted these girls to know that I valued them, so I began by appreciating their creativity. Then in order to help them think about the problem instead of feeling defensive about their behavior, I asked them why they thought it was so hard for "some kids" to stop working. I was saying that I knew that this was a common problem. This allowed the girls to respond as experts on childhood, instead of as guilty miscreants. Then I said that I, too, had the problem: I told them that when I'm writing, I often don't stop to eat. But the universality of the issue didn't mean that the girls were off the hook. They still had to figure out a way to freeze. I generalized their experience not to breed excuses, but to get them working on the problem. I believe that these things freed Julia so that she could move away from resistance to work on the issue in a meaningful way.

Sharing responsibility

I had had a management technique that worked for this problem. One could even say that my old way of addressing this worked better, since the new way only worked right away with one of these girls and even with her not all of the time, whereas I'd had almost 100% quick success with the other method. I tried something new because I had come to see my past successes as hollow. The children who had learned to freeze when I had used the old method hadn't learned to volunteer their ideas in the exchanges during freezes. They did the superficial freezing behaviors in order to avoid the humiliation of coming and standing next to me. While I gained external control, I also increased internal resistance. There was no growth in the bond that is so necessary for people to learn from each other. This old method was efficient but not effective.

The opposite was true with Julia. She invented a solution that made sense to her. It sprang straight from her hyperbolic style and, in fact, was very much on the mark in terms of the meaning of freezing. Because she thought of it and because it was so germane, she was invested in it and it helped her not only to listen during freezes but also to contribute.

"THIS ISN'T A PLACE FOR BABIES"

Julia's egocentric desire to do whatever she wanted was not limited to freezes. It got in the way of her friendships and her work. She and I dealt with this issue a great deal in the course of that year and by June, though the leopard hadn't changed her spots, she had made progress.

During the next to last week of school the class was working in math on story problems that combined addition, subtraction, and multiplication in very complex ways. It was challenging work but I felt that the children could get it and that when they did they would leave second grade feeling very accomplished in math. Math was the only academic skill that didn't come readily to Julia. But she hadn't given up on the extremely difficult problems that we were working on and eventually she was able to figure them out. I used her efforts as an example for the children of the way in which persisting could pay off with hard problems. Then on Thursday of that week, things took a dramatic turn for the worse for her.

The children were working on the problems in groups of three. I was helping a trio who had struggled mightily all week and who on this day had been able to move from despair to frustration to clarity because they had continued asking each other how they were thinking about the problem that they were working on. Their persistence in sorting out why they disagreed was bringing all three to exciting breakthroughs in their thinking. While I was working with this threesome, Julia's group came to me. Julia's partners were Toshika and Kelly, who were close friends. They said that Julia wasn't helping them think, that she was just doodling. Julia said that she needed to draw to be able to think. I told them that they had succeeded the past couple of days and that they could do it again, and I sent them back to work. A few minutes later they returned with the same complaints about each other and I repeated my earlier advice. A little later their continued fussing distracted me from the thrilling work with the breakthrough bunch. Toshika and Kelly were nagging at Julia, who was continuing to draw, an ugly pout on her face.

I thought, *Julia figured out the problems earlier this week when I was working with her group. She has to learn to do it without me there. She's being so obstinate about her drawing. She's still so self-centered—and manipulative.* I said, "Julia, you have to get back to work."

At this, she burst into tears. I ignored her. She raised the level to melodramatic sobbing. "Julia," I said, "this isn't a place for babies." Josh immediately called her a baby. I got on his case. He rightfully challenged me. This had rapidly become classroom quicksand.

At the end of math time, Julia calmly initiated conflict resolution with me (the only time a child has ever done such a thing). "You didn't listen to my side," she said.

"You're right," I answered. "I'm sorry."

"It felt like when my mom calls me a brat." She wasn't whimpering or whining about this. She was dry-eyed, clear, and strong.

"I shouldn't have put you down," I said. "I'm very sorry. Do you know why I got so mad?"

"Because of my crying."

"You're being incredibly strong and clear right now. I like this way of telling me what you don't like a lot better."

That night I decided that the combination of Julia, Toshika, and Kelly had become too problematic. I wanted them to end the year feeling good about math. I decided that for the last two days of math I'd find them more productive partners. Then I stopped short. *Wait a minute,* I thought. *I'm supposed to be trying to help them fight through their difficulties in math* AND *their problems with each other.* I resolved to help them work together.

At the start of math time on Friday, Toshika said she wanted to work with someone else. She said she couldn't figure out the story problems with Julia because they just fought all the time. I said that I wanted them to try to work together again and that I would help. Toshika gave a big groan. I asked all three of them, "What's making it so you can't work?"

Toshika responded immediately, "Julia just doodles."

"That's the way I think," Julia shot back.

Toshika said, "I try to explain what I think and you just say, 'I don't want to hear. I just have to do it myself.'"

"I need to think on my own to figure things out," Julia said.

Toshika fumed for a bit. Then she said, "How about if you have five minutes to think and then we talk?"

Without missing a beat, Julia said, "I need more than five minutes."

"I didn't mean five minutes exactly," Toshika said. "I meant when you're done thinking."

I said to Julia, "Toshika is being pretty flexible."

Kelly raised another issue. "Even if Julia has extra time, she'll still whine." Toshika seconded this.

I said to Julia, "They are willing to give you more time to think but they don't want you to whine."

"It's hard for me," Julia whined. "It's a habit."

I said, "Well, you've heard what they want."

"I'll try," Julia said.

I left them to work together, watching out of the corner of my eye. In two minutes, Toshika and Julia were talking over the story problem. They steadily became more animated and excited. Soon they brought me the results of their work. They both had a clear understanding of this very complex problem. After they explained their ideas to me, they went back and helped Kelly work on the problem.

From blaming to not blaming

In the first half of this story, I set out after my main goal—that the girls invent solutions—but I ignored the prerequisite steps that could make it happen. Instead of allying and wondering with them, I blamed Julia and told them to get back to work. I made no effort to get beyond my negative assumptions about Julia. I was stuck in my notion that she was selfish—and that her stubbornness was taking me away from other exciting work. The story comes to its happy ending in part because I switched from assuming that I knew what the problem was and telling the girls what to do about it to wondering with the three of them just what was going on and how it could be made better. Then when Julia persisted in her resistance, instead of dwelling on it, I just pointed out what Toshika and Kelly wanted from her and trusted that she would take it in, if not that day, then after some more repetitions.

My different attitudes were each very contagious. When I was judgmental and blaming, Julia got blamed by others. When I made it clear that I thought that there were more sides to the issue than Julia's personality flaws, Toshika became flexible.

Sharing responsibility

I think that three factors moved these girls to take responsibility for solving their problems. First of all, I insisted on it. Like the sixth grade soccer players, they were ready to give up. I myself had flirted with the idea that this was too difficult for them and not worth the effort. But I decided that though it would be hard for them to figure out how to work with each other, it was an important thing for them to try and it was not out of their reach. So I did not flinch when they began our discussion with groaning and complaints about each other.

I think that the second factor that helped them resolve things was that they got to air those complaints, to wonder about them together. The dynamic here reminds me of what I learned from Mrs. LaBelle and the playground tattlers. As in that situation, the change from having ideas and positions dismissed to having them acknowledged allowed these girls to speak out and then to move on. Having our experience accepted and appreciated for what it is often gives us a different perspective and also the incentive to try something new.

The third ingredient in bringing about the change in this story is that Julia and I believed in each other. Though I behaved poorly, she knew from experience that I would eventually listen to what was going on for her if she kept trying to tell me—especially if she could tell me without whining. For my part, I believed that Julia wanted to learn and to have friends, so I didn't make a point of her resistance. I think that it worked because Julia and I had been wondering about these issues together all year.

By the time he began second grade, Josh was an outcast. His motor ran a couple of r.p.m.'s faster than his peers' motors did and his inhibitions were less than theirs. This combination of speediness and impulsivity had alienated him from all of his classmates. I was his teacher for second grade. We had our ups and downs through the fall, but by December I had become thoroughly devoted to this troubled boy. I supplied great amounts of structure and nurturance and worked with the class around his pariah status and by late winter he was generally accepted and appreciated, had made a friend, and on many days was calm, productive, and friendly.

I then began to wean him from some of the systems that we had in place to help him stay grounded. I wanted him to begin to monitor himself more and also to begin to *choose* ways to help himself stay in control. One such effort toward greater autonomy centered around his meeting behavior. He had a habit of speaking whenever he felt the need. Early in the year, noticing that he could readily pay full attention to two things at once, I had given him a sketchbook to use at meetings. (He was a remarkable artist.) This helped a great deal, but he still interrupted too often. So together we decided that we would keep track at morning meeting of how often he talked out of turn, he in his sketchbook and I in my meeting notebook, and that he would try to keep the count at two or under.

Of course, there were periods of backsliding in Josh's effort to be in control. In March he was sick for several days and the morning he returned, he reverted to his old zooming self. He was zipping here and there and yelling across the room. A boy with a sprained ankle hobbled by and Josh grabbed a crutch. At writing time he knelt on his chair and sprawled across the table. Several of his papers were lying on the ground. When I went over to talk to him he slunk from his chair to the floor and slithered away on his belly. Maria said that he had just changed the name on Joel's writing folder from Joel the Dog to Joel the Frog. (Joel loved dogs and called himself Joel the Dog.) "He thinks it's funny, and it's not," Maria said hotly. I asked Joel if he wanted Josh to make this up to him in some way but Joel said that he could just change the name back.

I went over to Josh and had him get up off the floor and sit in a chair. "Look at these," I said, showing him my hands. They were red and raw, even cracked in some places.

"Why are they like that?" Josh asked.

"I have a skin problem that makes my hands itch and when I scratch them, they get like this."

"Why don't you stop scratching them?"

"I'm trying to learn to stop. But they itch so badly."

"You could wear gloves."

"That's an idea. Kind of uncomfortable to teach in them, though. But I could say to myself that if I scratched more than twice a day, I'd have to put on the gloves. Maybe that would help me want to stop."

"Why don't you just stop?"

"It's just very hard for me to control my scratching. I'm a little better than I used to be. I'm trying. Maybe your idea will help me some more. And you could help me another way. If you see me start to scratch, you could remind me that I shouldn't."

"OK," he said.

"There are times when you have trouble being in control. I'll keep a look out for those times; and you can let me know when you feel things slipping so that I can help you out. And you'll have to find ways to remind yourself, like I'm trying to do with my scratching." I paused. "I checked with Joel and he said that this time he doesn't want you to make it up to him for writing on his folder."

Later that day Josh was due to continue a block project that he had started in the morning with Charlie. I reminded him that he and Charlie had fought a lot about the building earlier. I gave him the choice of going ahead and seeing if a fresh start would help or of having me listen while he talked with Charlie about what didn't work in the morning. He chose to have me come and listen. After a little squabbling and a little help, they resolved the morning's problems and got to work.

In the afternoon we were about to start a math meeting that involved learning a game with bean bags. I was worried that this was going to be too stimulating for the barely-settled Josh. Generally, he only used his sketch book for the morning meeting. I asked him if he thought he might need it for this math meeting. "I don't need it," he responded. "I *want* it."

The relationship between blame and taking responsibility

At several points earlier in the year I had restricted Josh in various ways for his wild man behaviors—loss of privileges, time in the principal's office, the usual sorts of things. While I thought that these things might help him, mostly I did them because I was frustrated or outraged and didn't know what else to do. They never helped. The only lesson they taught Josh was that he was failing again; plus they got in the way of our creating any bond that we could build on. I gave up on these restrictions when a colleague helped me see how counter-productive they were. In their place I substituted more nurturance—and also more talk.

This March day was one that might have had me at my wits' end earlier. Wrecking someone's things doesn't go down easily with me; and then there were all the other wound-up behaviors. But when I looked over and saw Josh slithering across the floor, I didn't see a destructive boy this time but rather one who was miserable, terribly ashamed, and out of control. I wanted to take the spotlight off his behavior, which he so clearly understood was abominable. It seemed that the focus needed to be on ways to keep from getting so out of control, not on the present manifestation of impulsivity. I came up with a concrete and non-judgmental question for us to wonder about—how I could stop scratching my hands. I wanted to help Josh move a little further along the road toward noticing when he might go out of control and toward seeing that he had the power to develop and choose ways to stop the slide. Later that day he had already made two such choices: asking for my help with Charlie and *wanting* to use his sketchbook to help himself at the math meeting.

That spring Josh and I had conversations about recognizing his trouble spots, and inch by inch his autonomy grew—with regressions, to be sure. In June we were talking about how one can know that someone likes you and he said to me, "Well, I know that you like me."

"How do you know?" I asked.

"You want me to be good, but you never blame me for things anymore."

From working with Josh I learned a tremendous amount about the effect that blaming has on a child's capacity to begin taking charge of his problems, and an equal amount about the tightrope act of setting standards without being judgmental. Once I no longer blamed him, Josh could appreciate that I expected him to get better at being in control.

THE ELEPHANT CLUB

Maddie and Emma had been close friends since kindergarten. But when two new girls, Sanura and Vicki, entered the class in sixth grade, their long-standing friendship came under pressure. Late in the fall, Maddie and Sanura grew to like each other and spent every lunch time indulging in the exuberant giddiness of their new friendship. Emma was miserable and angry, but after a while the three of them worked things out and wound up all being close. Then in the winter Maddie and Vickie became tight. In response, Emma became very possessive of Sanura. The girls soon began to focus less on the pleasure of each other's company and more on the issue of who was liked by whom. The ramifications of these insecurities began to seep out to the other girls in the room. I was working part-time in this classroom and the lead teacher and I began feeling like we had wandered onto the set of a day time soap opera. Things boiled over when Maddie and Vicki decided to start the Elephant Club. Everyone could join as long as they gave the signal—an arm swinging from the nose like an elephant's trunk. Of course, it wasn't clear that everyone was invited or what the signal really was. Whispering and surliness quickly took over the room. The lead teacher, Margaret, and I met and devised a plan of what to do.

The next day, Margaret met with all the girls in the room. She told them that when she was in junior high school there had been a Silk Scarf Club. Her mother wouldn't let her get a silk scarf. Margaret went around telling everyone how stupid the club was. One day she got in an argument with a club member and she grabbed the girl's scarf and ripped it. "There," she said. "Now it's the Torn Scarf Club."

Margaret then told them another story, this time about when she was in fifth grade. She loved to do goofy things with her best friend, Lois Kurinsky. They traded a sock every day; at lunch they played soccer with their milk cartons under the table. They were always together. Finally her teacher made it clear to Margaret that she felt that the girls were bonding too much. Margaret was furious.

Margaret then had the girls write about a time when they had felt like insiders or outsiders. When they had finished Margaret asked if anyone wanted to share something they had written. After a couple of girls had read, Emma raised her hand, but then she said, "No, I don't want to."

"That's fine," Margaret said.

"Oh well, OK," Emma said. "I'll read it. 'For a while this year the only person I hung out with was Maddie. It probably wasn't fair of us to exclude other people, but then I didn't care. I know it made Liza feel as bad as it is making me feel about Maddie and Vicki.'"

Margaret said, "It's a really hard question for me, whether it's ever all right for friends just to be together and not welcome others. Some parts of me say yes and some parts say no. I'm not sure what I think."

Hannah said, "Excluding people is OK, but the way you exclude them is what's important. Like saying nicely that you don't want to play. Sometimes I don't want to share my friends, but I also know that's kind of mean."

"Clubs always end up with two groups mad at each other," Emma said.

"A group or club is OK," Megan said, "as long as it's just a bunch of kids who enjoy having fun together. Fights break out almost always among groups only around the thing of 'to include or not to include.'"

"It seems like a great idea at first," Vicki said, "but after a while including and excluding is what it all becomes about. It all turns sour. A club is an extremely bad idea."

Megan refined her earlier idea. "Clubs are OK, but clubs that meet are not. It's OK to know that you are part of a group, like the Worm Squishers, but when a club has meetings, that's bad."

"Clubs are OK, even secret meetings are OK," Sanura said, "but not *obvious* secret meetings."

Liza said, "It's even secretly delicious when others want to be part of your clique. It feels good because it's bad. A group of friends is good because then you know who to trust. It's not as fun when you start to add others because more fights start."

"Always, always, always someone gets left out when there are friends' groups," Vicki said.

Liza countered, "It's basically impossible to have friendships without having groups of some sort. Isn't it our right to have friends?"

The discussion went around and around. The girls kept saying that if it were such a strong human desire, one that everyone has, then how could it be that bad? But then someone would immediately remind the group about how bad it feels to be outside. Although no clear conclusions had been arrived at in this discussion, the budding hostility among the girls evaporated and they began to mix much more freely with each other. And they had the frankness and trust of this conversation to work from when this sort of problem came up again as the year went on.

Avoiding blame

I am often all too eager to seize the high ground on moral issues. Selfishness, dishonesty, aggression, and exclusivity are odious to me. Yet I know that I have all these qualities in me. Often it is only through admitting these impulses that I can avoid acting on them. But I can only acknowledge such things to a non-judgmental audience. When I am blamed, I'll defend myself. Margaret's vivid examples of how she had both exclusive and inclusive impulses in herself allowed these girls to explain and share what the experience of these two drives was like for them.

Sharing responsibility

Growth and resolution came about in this case even though the discussion was inconclusive and there was no action plan. Does this contradict the notion that an important part of what I have to do is to help children make responsible choices from among the possibilities that come up during our wondering? I don't believe so. I have come to think that responsible choice does not always depend on selecting a course of action. Sometimes it does seem best to urge a plan of action or to help formulate one. For example, I urged Josh to find ways to remind himself to be in control and I helped Julia devise a plan that would help her freeze. But in many situations—such as this one with the sixth grade girls—action plans get in the way of choosing responsibly because they focus on guilt over one's own actions rather than on taking others' needs into account. For example, after talking with Julia and Toshiko and Kelly about the difficulty they were having working together in math, I sent them back to their work without helping Julia plan how she would keep from whining. I just summarized what had happened in the conversation: that Toshiko had been flexible about Julia's needs and that she didn't like her whining. I have found that the parties in a conflict are most likely to be able to change if they work to know each other's stance more clearly. Too much focus on immediate action often leads to defensiveness rather than change. When, however, the exchange of views has been tried several times and has not borne some fruit, then it helps me to combine the wondering with an action plan. This was the case with both Julia's freezing and Josh's lack of self-control. I believe that the sixth grade girls increased their understanding of their complex problem and their connection to each other more by listening to each other's experience than they would have if Margaret had pursued with them some sort of action to address the situation.

These stories, in addition to being about responsibility and blame, are also about how to invite children to talk about difficult subjects. Although children may strongly prefer not to talk about something, they will often change this notion and even eagerly pursue a topic if I truly value and welcome their thoughts about the subject. I believe that one reason that my math students are very involved and invested is because I am always asking them for their thoughts about the problems.

In each of the examples in this chapter, I begin by seeking the children's expertise about the issue. When Margaret made it clear to the sixth grade girls that she saw both the reasons to exclude and those to include and that she wanted to hear their ideas on this thorny issue, they were off and running. Valuing children's ideas and inviting them to talk about them almost invariably opens up a conversation. In order to wonder together with children, I have to value their thoughts.

The children in these stories changed in small but important ways. They backed away from selfishness, stubbornness, impulsivity, and manipulation in order to try out some different possibilities. They were able to try these new things in part because their teachers did not judge them because of their mistakes but rather insisted that they work hard on creating solutions to their problems.

CHAPTER 6

Hunting Down

the Urgent Issue

A STORY ABOUT
SNAKES AND RATS
AND A BAD DAD

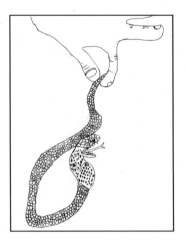

IN THE SITUATION WITH THE SOCCER OUTLAWS THAT I described earlier the real question that was at issue pretty much hit me over the head. I didn't have to think very long to figure out that the dilemma was about how to satisfy apparently contradictory needs. Since defining the problem came readily, I spent most of my energy allying with the boys and helping them take responsibility. The real issue that is at play is not always so apparent to me; when this happens more of my efforts go into tracking it down. Such was the case in the following incident.

Jenny was afraid of snakes. She also had an aversion to boys. There had been a particularly unruly pack of them in her kindergarten class and by second grade she hadn't yet recovered. One day near Halloween Jenny came to me and said, "The boys are talking about snakes around me and they know I don't like it."

I said to her, "You'd better really let them know what you think about that." This response might seem a little simpleminded, but I want second graders to become more resolute about tackling their conflicts with each other without a lot of adult intervention. For this reason I work hard to teach them conflict resolution skills. But my response in this situation was too facile for a different reason: my own pet aversion to whiners was at work. I told myself that I was taking away the soapbox Jenny needed to get full satisfaction from her victim status. With that in mind I could pretend to myself that I thought that something might come from suggesting that she challenge the boys, but somewhere in me I must have known how unlikely it was that she would follow up on this. What was most true was that I just didn't have many tools on hand to deal with her whining.

But that night the weakness of my response kept nagging at me. I had left this tattling girl and these teasing boys unprotected from each other and from themselves. They would continue to feed off their destructive expectations of each other unless I could somehow help them to interrupt the cycle. I had to try to help them move their dynamic onto a more fertile ground than the martyr and tormentors' place where it was now lodged. To make a beginning I had to figure out what the real question here was: I had to uncover "the urgent issue that connects us" (Paley, 1990, p. 106). In hunting for a universal human emotion underlying the situation, I came up with fear. I decided to see if exploring this angle at meeting the next morning might provoke some different interactions.

I started by reading them a seminal work on the pains and pleasures of being afraid, Arnold Lobel's "The Shivers," from *Frog and Toad All Day*. Then we talked for a while about ghost stories and severed heads and found out who liked such things and who didn't. (Besides me there were three or four children who didn't.)

Then I said, "Halloween is a time to have fun with scary things. But most people are also *really* afraid of some things. What do you think I might be afraid of?"

"Heights?"

"Muggers?"

"Wolves?"

"No," I told them. "I'm afraid of rats." They were aghast. Their big strong teacher afraid of rats?! "And," I continued, "anything like rats—mice, gerbils, hamsters."

They were sure that I was kidding them. *They* weren't afraid of rats and gerbils. A couple of them had mice for pets. How could I be afraid of them?

"Because when I go to sleep, they wake up and creep and sneak around everywhere. I've seen holes they've eaten in walls

and doors. There are so many of them. And they carry diseases."
I told them about my experiences with rats when I lived in Korea: how they thundered above me on the rice paper ceilings as I tried to sleep, how I opened my bottle of milk one morning and found a drowned baby rat, how a poisoned rat had paralyzed my dog. "They give me the creeps so bad," I said, "that I hate to even hear the word. Really. If my family has to talk about them, they say tar—that's rat spelled backwards."

When I now asked what they were afraid of, they were ready. Tough guy Charlie volunteered first—he was afraid of dogs *and* spiders. For Kate, it was things under her bed. I told how when I was a kid, the light switch in my bedroom was by the door, and at bedtime I used to switch it off and then run and leap into bed so that no arm could reach out and grab me. Many children told of similar and more elaborate techniques for getting to bed safely. Jenny brought up snakes. Jack hated the Ferris wheel. The stories continued and when it was time to go to math, many hands were still in the air. A good, healthy empathic airing, I thought. That should help.

An hour later, Jenny came to me distressed again. Maria had brought a rubber snake to school. It was part of Maria's Halloween costume and she was going to a party from school. "She told me that it was in her cubby so that I wouldn't get scared if I saw it. But Josh found it and put it in my face."

When there was trouble Josh was frequently fingered, and often enough the blame was at least somewhat justified. He usually had a hard time around holidays and his imagination especially feasted on the ghoulishness of Halloween. Evidently his impulses had not been stayed by my attempt to generate some empathy based on our similar fears. When I called him over, he said that there was a "gang" involved. After a little research, I found out that other boys had been involved. I had to deal with this situation and this time I wasn't going to have the luxury of some time alone to mull things over to uncover the urgent issue. I would have to do it on the spot, working from the skeleton of my principles: I'd have to pose the issue in a real and non-blaming way so that we could all stay curious enough to keep discussing the problem. During that discussion, I would have to listen carefully to try to hunt down the basic human issue at work and then try to frame it in a way that would help us come up with possible solutions.

I told the children that we had a problem and that I wasn't sure what I thought about it. We would put off science for a bit so we could talk about it. "The first thing I want to do in trying to figure this out is to get back to the discussion we were having this morning about things we are afraid of. So many of you had more to say."

Angela's hand shot into the air. "I'm afraid to go out and lock the chickens in at night. I think something might be waiting for me in the chicken house."

"Something like that happens to me," I said. "Sometimes I'm afraid to go upstairs at night."

Josh said that he was afraid of going into his basement because a tar might bite him. Tars lived down there and one had bitten him once. Though I guessed that this was probably an invention, the fact that he was talking about his fear and also allying with my fears seemed more important than literal truth.

Next, Sarah told about a movie that had scared her. Sean said that at camp last summer he had gotten scared by a counselor's campfire story. When Sean told us this, something clicked for me and I began to have a sense of what another key element in this situation might be. "Did the counselor know that he scared you?" I asked Sean.

"No. Most kids thought it was great. I couldn't sleep that night."

"I wonder what he would have done if he'd have known that he had scared you."

"Probably nothing," Sean said. "The story was supposed to be scary." Other children agreed with Sean that the counselor probably wouldn't have done anything.

I said, "I have a story about a time when I was like that counselor, only worse. A couple of years ago when my sons were eight and four, I was riding in the car with them around Halloween time and they asked me to tell a story. I made it one of those kinds where it's all spooky and quiet near the end. They could tell what was coming and they both asked me not to make a sudden loud ending. I agreed. But then I got carried away and did it anyway. I wanted to scare them and I did. They were really upset. I felt horrible. Now we always remember Halloween at our house as The Day Dad Was Bad."

I let the story hang in the air for a little bit and then I said, "Sometimes people want to do something that will hurt someone else, but they control themselves. That time I didn't control myself. That mistake made my boys feel so bad and made me feel so bad that I've been able to control myself about things like that since then." I paused again. Then I said, "Let's say someone in our room was like me that time. They couldn't control themselves. They scared someone. What could make that situation better?"

Several different versions of "say-you're-sorry" came forth. I validated each one and then, changing my role from fellow human and facilitator to gentle taskmaster, I kept asking if there might be anything else someone could do. They kept escalating the intensity with which you could say that you were sorry. Ownership of mess-ups was a fine lesson for them to take from this discussion, but I didn't want it to end there. After seven "say-you're-sorry" suggestions, Zack said, "If someone was really scared, I don't know if saying that you were sorry would really help that much."

Josh raised his hand. "If I scared her, I could draw her a picture." This was the first time that the actual incident that had provoked all this had been mentioned; and even now, it was done so only obliquely. Josh's suggestion did not spring purely from his creative generosity. Several weeks earlier I had suggested to him that since he was a skilled artist and that since he sometimes did things to people that he later regretted, he might think about drawing something for a classmate if he offended one. Though I had seeded this notion in Josh, he is the one who related it to this situation and chose to bring it up.

Jack then said that you could offer the person that you scared to tell you a scary story in return. David said they probably wouldn't want to do that since they didn't like scary things. But then Jack said, "Well, then you could do the opposite of a scary story for them."

"A joke," Sarah said. "You could cheer them up by telling them a joke." They were all delighted with the logic of this idea.

Jenny then said that she didn't mind if kids talked with her about snakes in a "nice" way as Maria had; she just didn't want to see them.

It was time to put all these ideas to the test. I said, "Anyone who was trying to scare Jenny this morning, go over to the round table and talk about it with her."

Five boys went over to the table with Jenny. Josh immediately offered to draw her a picture of a witch. Jackie told her a joke. Then Sam said, "I don't know what I could do. I'm not very good at drawing. I could tell you a joke, but I don't know any good ones. Oh, I know! I'll work with you in drama and we can make up a funny show!" The two other boys wanted to join in on the project and Jenny happily agreed.

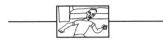

The breakthrough at the end of this discussion seems significant to me, certainly beyond what I had imagined would happen. The children built their success with this problem on the foundation of the real question which I was eventually able to construct for them. I finally realized that this incident had less to do with the universality of fear than with what to do about mistakes—how to admit to them, how to make amends, and how to offer forgiveness. The children molded these understandings into forms that made sense to them, finally even devising a very sophisticated form of reconciliation—the antagonists working together. In my teaching (and parenting) career, I have presided over so many meaningless, forced apologies. How did this situation end with such a genuine resolution? What set the stage for those five boys to march over to the table with Jenny and take real responsibility? What made her welcome their efforts? I believe that the answers revolve around uncovering the "urgent issue" and avoiding judgment.

After my initial blunder with Jenny, I had to work to depolarize the dynamic so that the participants might have a chance to work on the problem instead of each other. Perhaps what stands out in this effort is more what I decided *not* to do than what I did. I figured that the issues of whining and teasing would just ignite defensiveness and anger all over the room, so I never even brought them up. Actually it's an exaggeration to say that I "figured" that out. I'm generally not quick, cagey, or clear enough for such figuring on the spot. So if I didn't actually think things through, how did I know to avoid the inflammatory issues? I relied on my belief in looking beyond annoying behavior to the needs that the behavior serves. I avoided feeling condemning of the tormentors, and after a while I was also able to move away from my judgment of Jenny. I tried to find the ground that might evoke some empathy, so instead of focusing on the teasing and tattling, I kept the group talking first about the issue of fear and later about the issue of what's to be done when we make mistakes. I never even brought up the incident until the very end of the discussion.

Dealing with this issue with the whole group rather than with the individuals involved also helped depolarize the situation. It seemed very likely to me that, though this class was fairly well versed in conflict resolution, that route would soon become quicksand for these particular children in this situation. But if I could help the group discuss teasing in a thoughtful, non-judgmental way, the children involved in the problem, instead of being pitted against each other, might gain some clarifying distance and valuable help with their difficulty. (I also brought the issues to the whole group because I thought that they were important to everyone and because working on this kind of problem helps children learn very complex thinking skills. I keep my ear to the ground for this kind of opportunity to help children develop those skills.)

Perhaps what did the most to help eliminate the poisonous effects of judgment from this discussion was my being able to find ways that I shared in the human weaknesses on display. I have already talked about the effect of being able to explore genuinely how I, too, have whatever flaw, propensity, or desire might be under examination. The power that comes from doing this is abundantly demonstrated in these two discussions. In trying to understand why children could possibly be acting the way they are, I have found that examining my own motivations in similar situations is often the key that opens the door. Bringing my own flaws into a discussion immediately humanizes the conversation and makes us all want to work hard on figuring out what's to be done.

In these second grade discussions, it became possible to admit to one's fears and mistakes because, after all, the teacher, too, was sometimes afraid and out of control and even cruel.

Tracking down the real issue was especially difficult in this case because there were so many possibilities: aggression, gang behavior, fears, taunting, whining, passivity, male/female animosity, holiday overstimulation, the role of the bystander, and so on. Such a range of possibilities seems common in classroom upsets. My job in such situations seems much like that of a news photographer who must select from the huge diversity of possible images the one that best captures the situation. The brilliant photographer, Henri Cartier-Bresson (1968, preface), said this about how he makes such decisions: "The important thing is to choose between [the facts], how to fix on the fact that bears the stamp of profound reality."

In the situation with the snake, I first chose to focus on fears as the most germane and powerful of the issues. It turned out that fear was not the "fact" that bore the "stamp of profound reality," but it was close enough to get us going. I have seen some teachers who can size up a situation brilliantly, much like Cartier-Bresson does with his photographs. But I most often have to depend on a real question to help me see things clearly. The problem that I posed to the children about fear fits well my definition of a real question: one which helps the children and me wonder together about that rich area between the known and the unknown. It stimulated discussion so that we could see further, and then once the discussion got rolling, my role could be that of "a kind of psychological observer and tactician" (Sarason, Davidson, Blatt, 1962, p. 73). In this role I was able to spot what seemed to be the deeper issue. My question about fear was designed to help us start wondering together; that wondering then provoked the more fundamental question.

I got my first hint of what the real issue was when Sean told his camp story, but it was a while before I understood the situation clearly enough to ask the children about possible remedies for being out of control. The insight that I got when Sean told his story came as an intuitive flash that lighted the way toward the story of my scaring my sons. Telling this story then led me to the question of what we could do when we lost control. In this conversation I didn't have time, of course, to map things out. In general, in these kinds of discussions, although I put a lot of thought into how they might evolve, it doesn't pay to try to outline them too specifically. Though this way of proceeding can often bring the discomfort of not knowing exactly where things are going, it is also true that the power and pleasures of this way of working often come from the uncharted discoveries.

Choosing the direction that I did meant that other issues got shortchanged. It's no accident that the discussion dealt more with the teasing than with Jenny's role. I am just less capable of dealing productively with whining. Jenny did profit from this way of proceeding. Whiners often cling steadfastly to their role as victim, but Jenny wound up instead working happily with the boys who had been the source of her martyrdom. This was temporary progress, though. I wasn't able to stay the course in helping her get more satisfaction from being strong than from being oppressed. I made some weak forays into this land with her, but mostly I gave my attention to others' needs. I never get to all the children in my charge. Some year I will take on a whiner.

The children learned many lessons from this experience. They discovered that we are all in the same boat when it comes to fears and making mistakes; that problems can be solved by working together; that it pays to listen to each other; that it can be helpful to admit our mistakes; that others' needs are important; that we can come up with brand new thoughts when we think as a group; that our fallibility carries responsibility; and that good results can come from sticking with the hard parts of a discussion. More concretely, the idea of making amends became a part of what could happen in our room when someone messed up. I believe that these lessons came about because I was able to find the urgent issue—without finding fault.

Here is how I would break down my handling of this situation according to the elements of my three practices:

ALLYING WITH CHILDREN

Believing in children

I believed that these children could move beyond tormenting and tattling.

Understanding children

Knowing these particular children to be very defensive and impulsive, I avoided what I thought would be a very combustible conflict resolution situation by bringing the problem to the whole group in as non-threatening a way as I could.

Knowing my similarities

I could think about this situation without blaming anyone because I knew that I can be afraid and out of control and can want to scare others. My saying these things about myself let the children work on the situation without being defensive.

POSING THE REAL QUESTIONS

I didn't need the issue to be crystal clear before getting to work on it, but I did need a question that could catalyze more clarity. The question about fear led to the problem of what to do about one's mistakes.

SHARING RESPONSIBILITY

Wondering together

Since I don't get to the heart of the issue all that often on my first try, my job during a discussion is to stay alert to the possibilities which a real question opens up. In this case, as in most, we did much wondering about the layers of the issue before we got to mulling over possible solutions. The thrill of the hunt, of trying to unravel the issues and of probing further, is what makes this work so exciting and satisfying.

Setting high expectations

I insisted that the children deal with their animosity and explore solutions that went beyond apologizing.

Helping children make responsible choices

I insisted that the solution be more than superficial and the children eventually responded with great ingenuity.

CHAPTER 7

When to Wonder?

When to Tell?

When to Do Both?

THROUGHOUT THIS BOOK I HAVE BEEN SAYING THAT I
have found that the best way to help children to learn and to behave well is to wonder with them instead of telling them how to
figure things out and what to do. But, in fact, I tell children what
to do throughout my teaching day. I don't just greet them every
morning saying, "OK, let's learn," and then wait to see what happens. I tell them to read chapter six, to line up for recess, to study
their spelling, to sit down and write. If their homework is not very
thoughtful or if it's messy or too short, I tell them to work on it
until it's excellent. I separate children who are talking instead of
working, silence the lunch room for five minutes when I feel it is
too noisy, devise "behavior plans." Some of these things I feel
much better about doing than others. I am always trying to refine
my understanding of when it is best to be directive, when it would
be better to ask questions and talk, and when I should do both.

Until recently I believed in and used the flagship of the directive methods, time out. I worked at doing it right: short, unobtru-
sive, not punishing. I even changed its name to "take a break." I
used time out as a reminder about the rules and as a reminder that
I was watching. It especially helped me in running the tight and
productive meetings that I set so much store by. Then in January
one year I was reading Vivian Paley's *The Boy Who Would Be A Helicopter* (1990) and I came upon a section that stopped me cold. Her
words leapt off the page, challenging my thinking, goading me to
re-examine my use of time out:

> How could "locking up" a child . . . be a substitute for reason
> and discourse? (P. 86)

[When you use time out] difficult children and perplexing situations are no longer looked upon as problems to solve; you create instead the usual classroom story in which punishment becomes a central issue in the drama. (P. 87)

Harmful acts are stopped, of course, but the absence of "or else . . ." means that the children and I can use each other's mistakes and misunderstandings as lessons in cause and effect. (Pp. 85–86)

But, I objected, time out gives children the space in which to redirect themselves. And, of course, when the behavior is repetitive, I don't use time out alone; I talk with children about problems that come up consistently.

It turned out that Ms. Paley, too, had debated the issue with herself—for five years. Then one year she "abruptly" and "unequivocally" told her class that she was going to stop using the chair: "'It doesn't do any good. . . . No one behaves any better after being in the chair. . . . It makes children sad and it makes me sad too'" (p. 89). She started searching for a consistent and positive replacement for time out that would allow children's "errors [to] be used as legitimate learning experiences" (p. 91). The strategy that she devised was to become more intimately involved in children's story telling, expanding their metaphors with stories of her own "to suggest alterations in behavior" (p. 91).

Vivian Paley's books have changed my teaching as much as anything that I have read, but I couldn't translate her ideas about using children's metaphors to my own efforts to help children understand themselves and gain control of their behavior. Her replacement for time out was too sophisticated for me—or perhaps too obscure. Her idea was terribly attractive. Wasn't it the same thing that I was trying to do in math and with real questions—to open up more possibilities for change by expanding the avenues of exploration? But, after all, I didn't use time out to punish. I was also quite sure that if I got rid of time out, the replacement for it would be chaos.

A week later, during morning meeting with my second graders, Lily spoke out-of-turn. Lily often had to take a break during meetings for talking out. When she looked at me to receive the take-a-break order this time, I frowned slightly at her and shook my head a little, letting her know that I'd noticed and that I didn't want her to do it again. After I did this, I said to myself, *OK, I'm going to try this. I won't use time out at morning meeting for a few days. An experiment. I won't even tell them.*

My experiment became so intriguing that I didn't end it in a few days; instead I soon expanded it to our other meetings. Then I stopped using time out altogether because I was finding out some surprising things that I wanted to understand. I found out to my horror that one of the main functions of time out for me was that it allowed me to avoid dealing with behavior that was too frustrating or difficult or mysterious. Time out let me pretend that I had dealt with the problem, that time out's succinct message— *You know that isn't allowed*—was sufficient. I also found out that I had been fooling myself in another way: I hadn't been truly dealing with recidivists. When I abandoned time out and therefore couldn't dispense with an irritation with two quick words, I was suddenly forced to think about what was really going on for the child and to figure out a way to communicate about it.

I'll use my responses to speaking out-of-turn at meetings to show two ways that my teaching improved when I stopped relying on time out. First, I became more resourceful about what to do about this unwanted behavior. I soon found myself able to distinguish between different kinds of talkers: the impulsive, the silly, those who were chatting with their neighbor, those who were showing off. I was able to adopt different responses for different types of talkers. I might talk with an impulsive recidivist outside of meeting and together we'd brainstorm what could help: perhaps sitting next to me for a while, perhaps a signal, maybe a system for keeping track like the one I had with Josh. Liza's talking out was quite specific; she had a hard time getting back on track after something humorous had happened. She had a sturdy ego and I found that I could call her back without damage if I used a light touch. With other, less secure children, I might have a very brief mid-meeting private talk. I began to ask children to pay close attention to whom they sat near, sometimes asking them to change places if they couldn't concentrate. Show-offs required more in-depth conversations at a private time. These techniques are not revolutionary; I had used them all before, but not without time out, and not as well. When I started using them consistently instead of time out, they changed the tone of my meetings and changed my attitude toward the children. I found myself more allied with those who repeatedly had difficulties. These children changed from being stumbling blocks to being part of my responsibility and I, in turn, began to require that they rely less on time out and take more responsibility for their behavior.

The second advantage of not using time out at meetings was that, instead of becoming more chaotic, meetings improved. Part of this must have been due to the more sympathetic connection between the children and me. I also now became aware of their need to chatter with each other at lively points in the meetings. I started to see times when what we were discussing at meeting was so engaging that talk would bubble up all around the circle. When I saw this happening, I'd say, "Take two minutes to talk this over." I had been so proud of my meetings before. They had been so productive, but they had become *too* shipshape. As the children loosened up, I found that I did too. With this increased connection and looseness, meetings became livelier without losing their focus.

Occasionally chaos would get a little toe hold. I remember the combination of spring fever and a grumpy teacher brought this about at a couple of meetings in May. The children who had had the most difficult time at meetings had worked hard and were in control, but giggles, whispers, and talking were leaking out from everywhere else. I asked them what we could do about it.

"Bring back take a break," Kate suggested. A majority of the class agreed with her.

"No," I said. "We got rid of take a break. All we have to rely on in our room now is talking and listening and taking responsibility. So how can we get on top of this problem at our meetings?"

We discussed what it was that was making the meetings difficult and what sorts of things we could do besides time out to help them improve. This discussion brought the reasons for listening to each other back to life and the chaos was banished. This reminded me of another important lesson I had learned from Vivian Paley, one about rules. One year she decided that she wanted to establish a rule that said, "You can't say you can't play" (1992). She had many discussions with the children about the implications of this new rule before putting it into place. In spite of all these preliminaries, she did not at all expect that her official establishing of the rule would bring an end to the discussions about it. Mulling over and debating what happens when we try to follow or to avoid a rule are what can give the rule its power. Ms. Paley used her authority to make sure that her new rule was followed and used her authority again to make sure that the rule was kept alive by discussing its effects.

When the second graders and I began wondering together

about what had gone wrong with our meetings and how to fix them, I told them that time out wouldn't be an option. Why didn't I listen to their desire for a return to time out? Many times children do want to be told what to do, to have things be simple and safe, to know what the limits are so that they can experiment within them. In this case I felt that those who wanted time out to return were doing so not because they didn't feel safe without it but rather out of habit. They had seen teachers using it to address misbehavior for the two and a half years that they had been in school and they had had only three months of experimenting with other methods. I thought that they needed more experience with the other ways of gaining control and I wanted them to tax their imaginations a bit about these other possibilities.

About a week later we were having a discussion about how our meetings had gotten better without reverting to time out. Molly, an eighth grade student who worked with us sometimes, happened to be in the room at the time. I asked her if she had gone to time out when she was younger.

"Of course," she answered.

"Did it help?" I asked.

"No."

"Why not?"

"Sometimes I'd be mad at the teacher because I didn't do what she thought I did. And if I had done something wrong, I'd space out and think about something else when I was in time out."

Perhaps there are children who are able to make better use of time out, but there was general agreement amongst the second graders that they did the same things as Molly when they went to time out.

I have mentioned two ways that my teaching has benefited from giving up time out. I now have to deal with behavior that I had been ignoring; and I have changed my expectations and come to tolerate a little more disorder as a fair exchange for greater connection and understanding. There is also a third benefit: giving up time out has made me deal more with my emotional responses to misbehavior. Where I often used to use time out to sweep an offense under the rug, I now ask myself, *Why is this bugging me?* Doing this helps in two ways. First, if I can figure out what is making me angry, I will usually understand the child better. Second, my emotions become part of the interaction with the child. I realize that the question of just how much freedom I should give my emotions in the classroom is a complex one. I don't want to use anger to control children; rather, I want to use reason and connection to help children gain control. I know that one of the uses of time out is to protect children from teacher anger, but I also believe that my emotions, my reactions as a person, are an important part of the connection that helps children learn self-control. Sheltering my annoyance behind the facade of time out removes the possibility of this connection. It is also true that without time out, inappropriate emotion can seep into my teaching, as it did in the situation with Julia's math trio. But I believe that such mistakes on my part need to be weighed against the cold emotion that often leaked into my sending children to time out, no matter how bland I tried to keep it. The dismissiveness inherent in time out further intensifies the chill of its negative emotional impact.

The main character in the Langston Hughes's (1963) short story, "Thank You, Ma'm," Luella Bates Washington Jones, sets strict standards about misbehavior, but uses the opposite of the time out approach. When a boy tries to steal her purse, she could easily have resorted to time out, that is, called the police. Instead she employs two of the methods that I discovered when I gave up time out. 1) Rather than distancing herself from the thief, she becomes very involved with him. 2) She uses her anger to give her strength in her confrontation with the thief and to communicate her values to him.

In the story, a fourteen-year-old boy tries to steal her purse but slips and falls in the middle of his attempt. The woman picks him up and holds onto him tightly.

> Then she said, "Now ain't you ashamed of yourself?"
> Firmly gripped by his shirt front, the boy said, "Yes'm."
> The woman said, "What did you want to do it for?"
> The boy said, "I didn't aim to."
> She said, "You a lie!
> By that time two or three people passed, stopped, turned to look, and some stood watching.
> "If I turn you loose, will you run?" asked the woman.
> "Yes'm," said the boy.
> "Then I won't turn you loose," said the woman.

She tells him his face is dirty and that she's going to take him to her house to wash it

> "Are you hungry?"
> "No'm," said the being-dragged boy. "I just want you to turn me loose."
> "Was I bothering *you* when I turned that corner?" asked the woman.
> "No'm."
> "But you put yourself in contact with *me,*" said the woman. "If you think that that contact is not going to last awhile, you got another thought coming."

She drags him to her house and finally lets go, but she leaves the door open.

> "You gonna take me to jail?" asked the boy, bending over the sink.

"Not with that face, I would not take you nowhere," said the woman.

She has him wash his face. She says,

"I were young once and I wanted things I could not get."
There was another long pause. The boy's mouth opened.
Then he frowned, not knowing he frowned.

The woman said, "Um-hum! You thought I was going to say *but*, didn't you? You thought I was going to say, *but I didn't snatch people's pocketbooks*. Well, I wasn't going to say that." Pause. Silence. "I have done things, too, which I would not tell you, son—neither tell God, if He didn't already know. Everybody's got something in common. So you set down while I fix us something to eat. You might run that comb through your hair so you will look presentable." (Pp. 64–67)

She feeds him dinner and talks about her job. She does not say anything "that would embarrass him." When she finds out why he had tried to rob her, she says, "You didn't have to snatch *my* pocketbook to get some blue suede shoes. You could of asked me."

When they're done eating she says, "Now here, take this ten dollars and buy yourself some blue suede shoes. And next time do not make the mistake of latching onto *my* pocketbook *nor nobody else's*."

The woman was angry about the boy's behavior and she let him know it very directly. She was extremely directive with him. But instead of distancing herself from him—which is what time out allowed me to do—she sees his misbehavior as initiating "contact." She makes sure that that contact is going to "last awhile" and that it is rich: she is strong, nurturant, empathic, respectful, and generous. These things could not have happened if she had chosen to use her anger to punish him or if she had sent him to the police. In dropping time out, I have found that I have increased my chances for having this richer kind of contact with children.

Because I liked the way that giving up time out involved me more with the children and helped me to get on their side, I soon began re-examining the way that I used other directive methods—from logical consequences to behavior plans to separating children who had a hard time working together. What I am finding out about these things is complex. I cannot have the unequivocal attitude that I have come to have about time out. I believe that the need for both security and freedom are powerful in the classroom and they require that I be constantly vigilant about how the choices I make in one direction or another affect both the children and me. So I am always watching what happens as I choose to tell or choose to discuss and I debate with myself.

One side of me says:

- I can't discuss all the problems that come up. There are too many other things to do. It's also just too wearing to discuss everything.
- I have to be able to claim my space on the planet, to be able to say, "Stop that." When I begin to feel powerless I am likely to become angry.
- It isn't fair always to hold the needs of the many hostage to the needs of a few. Individuals have responsibility to the group.

My other side argues back:

- Talking is more productive in the long run—not the painful power struggles where I am trying to convince a child to see the light, but rather conversations where the child and I explore issues that can open up new possibilities.

• Connection helps people change more than the reasoned logic of rules. Connection comes from the combination of caring and conversation. When I talk with children instead of telling them what to do, I work harder to understand them. This creates more caring and connection.

What I have learned through this debate is that while I often find need for directives, I have been depending on them too much to bring about changes that only conversation and connection can effect. So now I try to substitute conversation for directives whenever I can. There are still lots of times when I choose to be directive, however. At those times I don't pretend that being directive is doing more than its share of the work of helping bring about change; and I try to examine why I've been directive and then to follow up on what I discover. But mostly I try to stay alert to whether wondering might work better than telling.

TIMES WHICH CALL FOR DIRECTIVE METHODS

I use directive methods to help maintain control; the children need a classroom where they are physically and emotionally safe and where they can do their work. While I try to replace directives with conversation whenever I can, I believe that behavior plans, logical consequences, and the like can be useful, not just as tools to help me keep control, but also in their own right. Two types of children, in particular, seem to benefit from directive methods: those with very low self-control and those who lack strength in particular circumstances. There are three situations when I use directive methods as one part of my efforts to help these children gain self-control.

I think learning can come downstream from doing when a desired behavior is very foreign to a child. Sometimes the ruts of habit can become so deep that there is no way for the wagon to get out of them other than to be lifted up and put elsewhere. I taught two fifth graders who had each pestered their classmates so much over the years that they had no friends. The year that I taught them was the first time that they had been in the same class and they latched on to each other. Their friendship, as you might guess, was ninety percent taunts and arguments. I talked with them about it. They both said that they wished that they didn't argue so much—and then fell to arguing about why it was that they argued. They were both avid scientists and a couple of their fights each day were over the microscope: who should use it when, how to use it best, just what they really saw in a drop of pond water. Finally I said that they could use the microscope each week as long as they did not have a single controversy about it. Within five minutes they had blown it, but they started over the next week. Soon they could last for days, then the week. Maybe, I figured, if they have fifteen minutes of peace each day around the microscope, they might experience each other in new ways and we could work at expanding on that.

One year I taught a third grader, named Rebecca, who was new to the school. She was charming, explosive, manipulative, clever, speedy, defiant, completely self-centered, and had no inner checks or balances. At her previous school she had often snuck out of the building when she was sent to the principal's office; she would hide out in a cemetery next to the school. In my room, she wouldn't follow any rules, was often selfish and nasty with other children, and wouldn't work—and she was an expert button pusher.

I worked hard the first month to stop the bleeding, then

started adding a rule a week to what I expected of her. During the winter I tried several varieties of checklists and rewards to help her follow these rules; these had only minor success. Then at the start of April, I hit on something that had a significant impact on Rebecca's behavior right through June. I broke the school day into eleven parts and listed them on a daily scorecard. She scored a point for every part of the day that she was able to follow the rules and be kind. We totaled each day's score at dismissal time. There was no reward connected to the scores; her father, who picked her up after school, just checked in on her total each day. For some reason, this combination of accruing points and her father's daily check-in motivated Rebecca and helped her gain some momentum in behaving a different way. There were many ingredients that went into helping her be happier and more socialized that spring and I think that this behavior plan was an important one.

I will not attempt to cover my experiences with the use of behavior plans in anything resembling scientific thoroughness. What I am urging is that we teachers watch closely the effects of the directive and non-directive methods we use and adapt accordingly. I have seen behavior plans be of no help to children at least as often as I have seen children gain from them. I used to have several children each year on plans. I now use them more sparingly. The following story illustrates why I am being more selective about using them.

I taught a fifth grader, named Eric, who had been on behavior plans in his first, second, and third grade years to help sensitize him to times when his behavior was offensive to other children. He would pull off someone's hat while waiting in line, "accidently" knock over someone's block building, that sort of thing. His fourth grade teacher dropped the behavior plan in September and instead confronted him about his behavior frankly and with humor. He developed a strong bond with this teacher and his behavior improved greatly. He did fine until early winter of his fifth grade year when he began to exhibit some of his old characteristics. He had also by then added a deadly sarcasm. Then one day he was nasty to a first grader in a very public situation. I was worried that Eric was developing a malicious side, but my co-teacher believed that he sincerely did not understand the effect of his acts and wondered if he might not be helped by the return to a checklist for a bit. We decided we would first see what happened when we talked to him.

We started our conversation with him by saying that we were worried that he was going to start alienating children again. We talked about sarcasm, about what makes it funny and what makes it offensive, and about impulses. Eric had had so many conversations with teachers about his behavior over the years that whenever such a talk became the least bit preachy or directive he tuned out or became dismissively compliant. But this time, because we began with concern and real questions instead of with a push or a plan, he was sincerely and thoroughly involved. Eventually we asked him how he would get on top of this problem. In response he delivered a brilliant, passionate, and precise diatribe against behavior plans, what he hated about them and why they didn't help him. We left it that he would just try harder. His nastiness stopped for a couple of months following this conversation, and when it showed signs of returning we talked again.

I still sometimes choose to use directive methods if I think they might give a child the chance to experience another side of herself. But I first try to think of what else might work.

Extreme Situations

Directive methods can also be intrinsically worthwhile when they help me stay calm in the face of very inflammatory behavior.

When a child like Rebecca does something outrageous or continues to push against the limits, I am able to be much less reactive if I can depend on a system which I have put in place to do the reacting for me. I spoke earlier about making a place for emotion in discipline, but here I am talking about keeping a lid on my emotion when the most troubled children are doing their extreme things. Directive systems by no means automatically take away my frustration and anger. But having a consequence to rely on gives me a better chance of staying calm. With the most provocative children I have to work extra hard to stay even or to keep my sense of humor. Logical consequences often provide me with a safety net in these efforts.

Group needs versus individual needs

We live our lives with others, and children without inner discipline often need help in taking others' needs into account. I find that logical consequences can help such children see that participation in a group requires that they become able to look beyond their own needs. I sometimes will establish the rules and consequences myself so that the children can get on with their academic and social labors. Often, however, I have the class set the standards and determine consequences when I judge that a group decision will be a better way for individuals to be responsive to the group's needs. Here are some examples of this:

• When a second grade girl grabbed a felt tipped pen from a classmate, I brought the issue before the class and they had a lively discussion about whether it was ever all right to grab something they wanted. There was much feeling and reasoning and refining on both sides, but they finally decided that it wasn't acceptable and set up a consequence for those who grabbed.

• I once had an extremely lively sixth grade reading group. Three-quarters of the children were opinionated and impetuous. All the talking-out-of-turn wore me down. When we discussed it, it turned out that they found it tiring, too. They came up with an ingenious way to monitor themselves: they would listen to each other, but if someone talked too long, they could interrupt by raising their hands. (They applied this to me as well.) The group went much more smoothly with this consequence in place.

• Part of a group of fifth graders whom I taught had to switch rooms every day for math. They usually got to the room a minute or two before I did and three of the children had a hard time with that amount of autonomy and made life miserable for the others. The group decided that it might help these children make the transition more smoothly if the first five minutes of math time could be spent doing something active (they proposed the game of Duck Wars); they also thought that anyone who showed they still couldn't be in the room without me would wait with me until I was ready to come. With these two consequences in place the transition problems disappeared.

I should add that I believe that there is one thing that is especially important to take into account when I involve the group in helping individuals take responsibility, something that is clear in these fifth and sixth grade examples. I try to focus the children on thinking ingeniously about what might help change behavior rather than on punitive consequences, which is where their minds (I should say our minds) tend to go first.

GUIDELINES FOR BEING DIRECTIVE

So in using directives, how am I any different from the sergeant who barks out orders?

- I try not to bark.
- I try to be very judicious about how often and just when I tell children to do things.
- I try to be like Mrs. Luella Bates Washington Jones: I try to use directives as a jumping off point to other kinds of help.
- I give my reasons for the limits I set.
- I often involve children in discussing and working out what the limits, plans, or consequences will be.
- I am willing to discuss the repercussions of the rules—the benefits and difficulties of following them.

Sometimes I just plain need the children to do what I say, to trust that I have their best interests in mind or that my limits have been reached. More often when I use my authority and employ directive methods, I try to use the above techniques to imbue my orders with reason and caring.

MIXING WONDERING AND TELLING

I've been treating wondering and telling separately but, in fact, classroom life doesn't allow for such tidiness. For example, I don't only give orders as a preliminary to conversation, but also often in the middle of wondering with children; and I also wonder with children while I'm setting limits. Then too, I always try to layer in the nurturance that helps children want to change. This brew of telling, wondering, and nurturing was true of my work with Rebecca. Besides using various consequences and checklists to help her move from surliness toward friendliness, I also wondered with her about whom she might want for a friend, and then I helped her talk with those children about what might make friendship possible. I also laughed at her jokes, talked quite a bit with her about Kimberly of the Power Rangers, gave her important classroom jobs, made extra time for her to do the art work she was good at and gave her plenty of hugs. The following is another more seat-of-the-pants example of mixing telling and wondering.

Josh, Charlie, and Rocky were playing together with some action figures in the block area but they were doing more fighting than playing. They had started with turf battles and then moved on to squabbling over the figures.

"That's mine."

"You grabbed it."

"You can't use that one."

I went over and asked what was going on and got a blizzard of opinions. To gain some clarity and peace I could have:

• Told them that they were being too disruptive and argumentative so they had lost their right to play in the blocks.
• Told them that they could continue as long as they didn't fight. If they fought, they were done.
• Let them continue, but separately from each other.
• Talked about sharing and playing together.
• Decided for them who could play with each figure.

I have tried all of these approaches many times in similar situations. This time I had them give me the figures and come over to a table away from the block area. I asked to whom the figures belonged. It turned out that five were Josh's, one was Rocky's, and none were Charlie's. I asked them, "How can we make this work?"

Charlie said, "Josh always decides who gets to use which one."

"And he always uses the best ones," Rocky said.

Charlie pointed at me. "You decide who uses which one."

"But what will happen if you don't get the one you want?" I asked. "How will it work out?"

"We'll just share them," Charlie said.

Rocky and Josh immediately agreed with this preposterous

notion. I expressed my disbelief. "But I haven't seen any sharing, only grabbing. How will this sharing work?"

Josh said, "We'll ask each other."

"Or trade," Rocky added.

I closed my eyes and handed out the figures randomly. As I did, I heard much "darn" and "yeah."

They went back to the blocks and I checked on them about five minutes later. Josh and Charlie were exchanging figures. Charlie noticed me and said, "Hey look, it works! Good trade, huh?"

Why the precipitous change from acrimony to pleasure? I was very directive: I stopped the boys from playing, moved them away from the block area, and made them give me the figures. But I didn't just close them down; I closed them down so they could talk things over and invent a solution. I kept alternating between telling and wondering. After the initial limit setting, I asked them, "How can we make this work?" Then I had them mull over the likely problems in their proposed solution. I wouldn't let them go back to the blocks until they had invented ways to play that could really work. I insisted that they create a solution and in the end, because *they* came up with it, they were invested in it working. I do not believe the same ending could have come about if I had gone over to where they were playing and randomly distributed the figures on my own.

The strong, wise, and generous Luella Bates Washington Jones is a good model of how to mix telling, conversation, and nurturing. She started being powerfully directive so she would have the chance to talk and nurture. Then after talking to the boy and nurturing him, she returned to being very directive about what he should do in the future.

I have wound up with these two guidelines for myself about mixing wondering and telling. I use directives to insist that children wonder and invent solutions; and I use them to set high standards for children to aim at as they wonder and invent.

Ultimately, the issue of how to blend telling and wondering and nurturing in teaching is so complex that it resists sweeping guidelines and instead insists that I spend a good deal of my teaching day refining my judgment about which methods will work best. I have to rely on my ability to watch what really happens, think things through, and care about children. The biggest help to me in this task is to keep my two goals clearly in front of me. Dozens of times every day, in one way or another, I ask myself these questions:

• Has my choice helped me to be on this child's side?
• Will my choice help this child invent a solution?

To answer these questions I have to be thoughtful and honest, always balancing the trade-offs that come with every choice. When Jonathan chatters while I'm explaining how to play a game and so I have him be the last to play, am I just distancing myself from dealing with his needs? Would taking the time for a few private words with him show him that I care about his problem and show the group that I care about everyone's issues or would it show them that I care about the needs of many less than the needs of one? Which choice will help Jonathan develop more control? Will calmly separating two bickering children protect them from my frustration with them, or would a little conversation and emotion on my part get us tuned in to things I have been skirting?

I also have to take into account just how many of these conversations I have the energy for each day. During a particularly trying week one year I wrote in my journal, "I have been spending so much energy trying to understand the children that I have no energy left for *being* understanding with them." Too much wondering had blotted out my nurturant side.

In the short story, "Terrific Mother," Lorrie Moore (1993)

writes: "Marriage soup. . . . It was perhaps a little like marriage it-self: a good idea that, like all ideas, lived awkwardly on earth" (p. 312). Theories about how best to help children learn and change have to be broad enough to encompass the vitality and ambiguity that come with life in a classroom. If relied on too exclusively, be-haviorism or constructivism or nurturance wind up "living awk-wardly" in school. They are more useful when they are blended well. Over the years of brewing many batches of classroom soup, I have found that to make it both rich and full of flavor, I need a broth of telling as the foundation for the spices of wondering and nurturing. Asking myself the two questions about my goals pro-vides a very exacting taste test. My recipe, which relies greatly on the ingenuity and resourcefulness of the cook, winds up looking like this:

- Wonder with children as often as possible.
- Use directives to insist on high standards for children's wonder-ing and inventing, to give a child the chance to experience an-other side of herself, and to get through the day.
- Continually reflect on how different choices will help achieve the goals of empathizing with the children and helping them in-vent solutions.

FINAL THOUGHTS

———

A K-I TEACHER TOLD ME A STORY ABOUT A VERY CURIOUS boy who frequently inspired learning in her classroom. He would ask, "Why does the snow melt on this side of the hill and not on that side?" or "What does the novocaine do in your mouth so the drilling doesn't hurt?" In June the teacher was helping the children think about what they had taught each other that year. This boy couldn't think of any way that he had helped someone to learn something.

"But, Zack," the teacher said, "what about all the times that you helped us discover things in science—like about the nerves in our mouths or about the tadpoles? Your questions help us figure out so many things."

"That's not teaching," Zack replied. "That's just wondering."

This powerful way of teaching was instinctive with Zack. For most of my career, this approach has not come naturally to me. When my class studied flowers, I told children all about the stamen and pistil whether they wanted to know or not. When Kate and Jabari put each other down, I told them to stop and that was usually as far as I got in trying to help them. Then from my work in science and math I learned about the excitement and power that comes from wondering with children about provocative questions. Now when we study flowers I have to journey far from the safety of the stamen and pistil, but I get to think with children about things like what makes the water go up the stem and why it is that burrs stick to us. Now I wonder with children like Kate and Jabari about what they get out of being on each other's case and if there is another way they might want to treat each other and how they could give it a try.

The questions that teachers most frequently ask about working in this way are: Does it work? How can I begin? And, isn't it harder?

The first year that I tried using constructivist math, my friend Deborah came into my second grade classroom on the third day of school to see how it was going. I had just put this problem on the board: 1 + 6 + 7 + 4 + 8. Deborah gave me a look of horror. "They can do this?" she asked. "Watch," I said, and they proceeded to solve the problem in four different ways. This method works; this book is full of examples of its efficacy.

There are many ways to begin experimenting with these methods. I began in science and then moved on to math. I cut down on using time out. I experimented with the way I talked with individual children about their behavior. I began working with the whole class to figure out possible solutions to problems that came up.

Although initially it was hard to change my way of thinking, once I made the switch, it was so satisfying that it soon became a habit. The new habit hasn't necessarily made my job easier. For one thing I now always have to decide whether to use the wondering habit or the directive habit. Also, when I try to find out how a child is thinking about a flower or about a feud with a friend, I immediately become intimately involved with her confusion and struggles. Helping a child sort through this sort of complexity doesn't make my job simpler, but it makes it enormously exciting. It also helps the child learn. Wondering with a child in this way puts me in the middle of her experience and it also allows me to be out of the way enough for her to have her own thoughts and to take charge of her life.

BIBLIOGRAPHY

ESSENTIAL

My teaching has changed a great deal in the past five years. The two books that have most influenced that change are *The Boy Who Would Be a Helicopter* and *Young Children Continue to Reinvent Arithmetic.* Though these books are extremely different from each other, I found them to be similar in the way that they provoked and challenged my thinking. I highly recommend both.

Paley, Vivian. *The Boy Who Would Be a Helicopter. The Uses of Storytelling in the Classroom:* Cambridge, MA: Harvard University Press, 1990.
Kamii, Constance, with Linda Joseph. *Young Children Continue to Reinvent Arithmetic—2nd Grade: Implications of Piaget's Theory.* New York: Teachers College Press, 1989.

PRACTICAL

Allying, asking real questions, and sharing responsibility won't even have a chance to happen unless I structure my classroom so it works. If I make the work for cooperative math groups too hard or too easy, the children are likely only to cooperate on making trouble. If the class makes a field trip to a pond and I haven't put enough energy into how we'll work out-of-doors, the field trip will probably include a lot of wet feet and a fair amount of sword-fighting.

Here are the books that have helped me develop the skills to make sure that my classroom is structured for success.

Three very thoughtful and practical approaches to the social curriculum:

Charney, Ruth. *Teaching Children to Care: Management in the Responsive Classroom.* Greenfield, MA: Northeast Foundation For Children, 1992.

Faber, Adele and Elaine Mazlish. *How to Talk so Kids Will Listen & Listen so Kids Will Talk.* New York: Avon Books, 1980.

Nelsen, Jane. *Positive Discipline.* New York: Ballantine, 1987.

The essential nuts and bolts of classroom management:

Charney, R., M. Clayton, M. Finer, J. Lord, and C. Wood. *A Notebook for Teachers.* Greenfield, MA: Northeast Foundation For Children, 1984.

Clayton, Marlynn. *Places to Start: Implementing the Developmental Classroom.* Greenfield, MA: Northeast Foundation For Children, 1989. 2nd Ed. 1995. (Videotape)

A clear, concise, but thorough guide of what to expect at each developmental age:

Wood, Chip. *Yardsticks: Children in the Classroom, Ages 4–12.* Greenfield, MA: Northeast Foundation For Children, 1994.

INSPIRATIONAL

Each of these books is brimming over with insight and inspiration. Consider reading and discussing one with a colleague instead of (or in addition to) attending a workshop next summer.

Bettelheim, Bruno. *Love Is Not Enough.* London: Macmillan, 1970.

Bettelheim, Bruno. *The Uses of Enchantment: The Meaning and Importance of Fairy Tales.* New York: Knopf, 1976.

Duckworth, Eleanor. *"The Having of Wonderful Ideas" and Other Essays on Teaching and Learning.* New York: Teachers College Press, 1987.

Duckworth, Eleanor. Twenty-four, Forty-two, and I Love You: Keeping It Complex. *Harvard Educational Review,* 61 (1), February, 1991.

Fosnot, Catherine. *Enquiring Teachers, Enquiring Minds: A Constructivist Approach for Teaching.* New York: Teachers College Press, 1989.

Hawkins, David. *The Informed Vision: Essays on Learning and Human Nature.* New York: Agathon Press, 1974.

Nicholls, John, and Susan Hazzard. *Education as Adventure: Lessons from the Second Grade.* New York: Teachers College Press, 1993.

Paley, Vivian. *You Can't Say You Can't Play.* Cambridge, MA: Harvard University Press, 1992. Paley's other six books are all excellent.

Piaget, Jean. *To Understand Is to Invent: The Future of Education.* New York: Grossman, 1973. Even if you've despaired of reading Piaget, give this one a try. It's quite accessible—and it's short.

Wadsworth, B. *Piaget for the Classroom Teacher.* New York: Longman, 1978.

ACADEMIC

If I had to choose one book for each of the basic curriculum areas, these would be the ones. Each covers all the elementary school years.

Holdaway, Don. *Independence in Reading.* Sydney: Ashton, 1980.

Calkins, Lucy. *The Art of Teaching Writing.* Portsmouth, NH: Heinemann, 1986.

Doris, Ellen. *Doing What Scientists Do: Children Learn to Investigate Their World.* Portsmouth, MA: Heinemann, 1991.

Burns, Marilyn. *About Teaching Mathematics: A K-8 Resource.* Sausalito, CA: Math Solutions Publications, 1992.

I have to list one extra math title:

Skinner, Penny. *What's Your Problem? Posing and Solving Mathematical Problems, K-2.* Portsmouth, NH: Heinemann, 1990.

REFERENCES

Cartièr-Bresson, Henri. 1968. *The world of Henri Cartier-Bresson.* New York: Viking Press.

Doise, W. and Mugny,G. 1984. *The social development of the intellect.* New York: Pergamon.

Doris, Ellen. 1991. *Doing what scientists do: Children learn to investigate their world.* Portsmouth, NH: Heinemann.

Duckworth, Eleanor. 1987. *"The having of wonderful ideas" and other essays on teaching and learning.* New York: Teachers College Press.

Duckworth, Eleanor. 1991. Twenty-four, forty-two, and I love you: Keeping it complex. *Harvard Educational Review,* 61 (1).

Duckworth, Eleanor. 1995. Personal communication. September 27.

Fosnot, Catherine. 1989. *Enquiring teachers, enquiring minds: A constructivist approach for teaching.* New York: Teachers College Press.

Hughes, Langston. 1986. *Thank you, m'am.* In Robert Shapard and James Thomas (Eds.), *Sudden fiction: American short-short stories* (pp. 64–67). Salt Lake City: Peregrine Smith Books.

Inhelder, B., H. Sinclair, and M. Bovet. 1974. *Learning and the development of cognition.* Cambridge, MA: Harvard University Press.

Kamii, Constance. 1985. *Young children reinvent arithmetic: Implications of Piaget's theory.* New York: Teachers College Press.

Kamii, Constance, with Linda Joseph. 1989. *Young children continue to reinvent arithmetic—2nd grade: Implications of Piaget's theory.* New York: Teachers College Press.

Kamii, Constance. 1989. *Double column addition: A teacher uses Piaget's theory.* New York: Teacher's College Press. Videocassette.

Kazin, Alfred. 1994. Jews. *The New Yorker,* 70 (2), pp. 62–74.

Kidder, Rushworth. 1995. *How good people make tough choices.* New York: Morrow.

Moore, Lorrie. 1993. Terrific mother. In Louise Erdrich (Ed.), *The best American short stories: 1993.* Boston: Houghton Mifflin, 300–334.

Nicholls, John, and Susan Hazzard. 1993. *Education as adventure: Lessons from the second grade.* New York: Teachers College Press.

Paley, Vivian. 1981. *Wally's stories.* Cambridge, MA: Harvard University Press.

Paley, Vivian. 1984. *Boys and girls: Superheroes in the doll corner.* Chicago: University of Chicago Press.

Paley, Vivian. 1990. *The boy who would be a helicopter: The uses of storytelling in the classroom.* Cambridge, MA: Harvard University Press.

Paley, Vivian. 1992. *You can't say you can't play.* Cambridge, MA: Harvard University Press.

Paraskevas, Michael. 1993. Where the heart is. *Teaching Tolerance,* 2 (2), 19–25.

Piaget, Jean. 1973. *To understand is to invent: The future of education.* New York: Penguin.

Prine, John. Far from me. *John Prine.* Atlantic 19156.

Sarason, Seymour, K. Davidson, and B. Blatt. 1962. *The preparation of teachers: An unstudied problem.* New York: Wiley.

White, T. H. 1993. *The sword in the stone.* New York: Philomel Books.

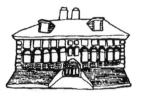

NORTHEAST FOUNDATION

FOR CHILDREN

Resources for Teachers

◆

Since 1985,

Northeast Foundation for Children

has published books on education

for those who believe in the importance

of developmentally appropriate practices

and a strong social curriculum

in our schools.

In addition to its publishing activities,

Northeast Foundation for Children

offers educational workshops and

consulting services and operates

Greenfield Center School,

a K–8 school in

Greenfield, Massachusetts.

Teaching Children to Care: Management in the Responsive Classroom
RUTH S. CHARNEY

Speaking to the heart of every classroom teacher, this book offers a proven, practical approach that helps reduce the exhausting and often overwhelming classroom management problems confronting today's K–8th grade teachers. *Teaching Children to Care* presents theory, practical guidelines, and real-life examples which show how to create classrooms where caring is practiced.

0-9618636-1-7/single copy $22.50/quantity discounts/paperbound/314 pages/1992

Yardsticks: Children in the Classroom, Ages 4 to 12
CHIP WOOD

This is the one quick and comprehensive child development guide teachers will want by their side. *Yardsticks* can help boost confidence and ultimately benefit students by comparing their behavior with documented milestones. Numerous charts and illustrations make this the perfect resource to clearly and concisely answer parents' questions too.

0-9618636-2-5/single copy $12.95/quantity discounts/paperbound/172 pages/1994

A Notebook for Teachers: Making Changes in the Elementary Curriculum
NORTHEAST FOUNDATION FOR CHILDREN STAFF

This timeless resource can help teachers integrate developmentally appropriate teaching techniques into the classroom. *A Notebook for Teachers* includes details on the behavior characteristics of 5, 6 and 7-year olds, as well as classroom implications. Includes over 150 charts, examples, photographs and illustrations.

0-9618636-0-9/single copy $19.95/quantity discounts/paperbound/78 pages/1993 ed., orig. 1985

Places to Start: Implementing the Developmental Classroom
WRITTEN, PHOTOGRAPHED & PRESENTED BY
MARLYNN K. CLAYTON

A classic in the field of developmentally appropriate practices, this video provides a wealth of practical, effective ideas that have been classroom tested over many years. These ideas work to create an active, productive, learning and caring classroom community.

$49.95/$59.90 with Notebook for Teachers/VHS/color/90 min./16pg viewing guide/1995 ed., orig. 1989